T R A N S F O R M I N G

UNDERGRADUATE

EDUCATION IN

SCIENCE,

MATHEMATICS,

ENGINEERING,

AND

TECHNOLOGY

Committee on Undergraduate Science Education
Center for Science, Mathematics, and Engineering Education
National Research Council

NATIONAL ACADEMY PRESS
Washington, DC 1999

NATIONAL ACADEMY PRESS • 2101 Constitution Avenue, NW • Washington, DC 20418

NOTICE: The project that is the subject of this report was approved by the Governing Board of the National Research Council, whose members are drawn from the councils of the National Academy of Sciences, the National Academy of Engineering, and the Institute of Medicine. The members of the committee responsible for the report were chosen for their special competences and with regard for appropriate balance.

The National Research Council (NRC) is the operating arm of the National Academies Complex, which includes the National Academy of Sciences, the National Academy of Engineering, and the Institute of Medicine. The National Research Council was organized in 1916 by the National Academy of Sciences to associate the broad community of science and technology with the Academy's purposes of furthering knowledge and providing impartial advice to the federal government. Functioning in accordance with general policies determined by the Academy, the Council has become the principal operating agency of both the National Academy of Sciences and the National Academy of Engineering in providing services to the government, the public, and the scientific and engineering communities. The Council is administered jointly by both Academies and the Institute of Medicine. Dr. Bruce M. Alberts, President of the National Academy of Sciences, and Dr. William Wulf, President of the National Academy of Engineering, also serve as chairman and vice chairman, respectively, of the National Research Council.

The Center for Science, Mathematics, and Engineering Education (CSMEE) was established in 1995 to provide coordination of all the National Research Council's education activities and reform efforts for students at all levels, specifically those in kindergarten through twelfth grade, undergraduate institutions, school-to-work programs, and continuing education. The Center reports directly to the Governing Board of the National Research Council.

This study by CSMEE's Committee on Undergraduate Science Education (CUSE) was conducted under a grant from the Exxon Education Foundation to the National Academy of Sciences/National Research Council. Any opinions, findings, or recommendations expressed in this report are those of the members of the committee and the authors and do not necessarily reflect the views of the Exxon Education Foundation.

Library of Congress Cataloging-in-Publication Data

Transforming undergraduate education in science, mathematics, engineering, and technology / Committee on Undergraduate Science Education, Center for Science, Mathematics, and Engineering Education, National Research Council.
    p. cm.
  Includes bibliographical references (p.).
  ISBN 0-309-06294-2 (perfectbound)
    1. Science—Study and teaching (Higher)—United States. 2. Mathematics—Study and teaching (Higher)—United States. 3. Technology—Study and teaching (Higher)—United States. I. Center for Science, Mathematics, and Engineering Education. Committee on Undergraduate Science Education.
  Q183.3.A1 T73 1999
  507.1'173—dc21
                        99-6151

Additional copies of this report are available from the National Academy Press, 2101 Constitution Ave., NW, Lock Box 285, Washington, DC 20055.
(800) 624-6242 or (202) 334-3313 (in the Washington metropolitan area)

This report is also available online at <http://www.nap.edu>

Printed in the United States of America.
Copyright 1999 by the National Academy of Sciences. All rights reserved.

Cover photos reproduced by permission:
    © Richard S. Mandelkorn
    © Department of Biology, Colby College
    © Jeffrey D. Marx
    © Arne Kuhlman, '97, Washington and Lee University

COMMITTEE ON UNDERGRADUATE SCIENCE EDUCATION

Current members

MARYE ANNE FOX (NAS*), University of Texas at Austin, *Chair*
MARY P. COLVARD, Cobleskill-Richmondville High School
ARTHUR B. ELLIS, University of Wisconsin, Madison
DOROTHY GABEL, Indiana University
JAMES M. GENTILE, Hope College
RONALD J. HENRY, Georgia State University
HARVEY B. KEYNES, University of Minnesota
PAUL J. KUERBIS, The Colorado College
R. HEATHER MACDONALD, College of William and Mary
GRACE MCWHORTER, Lawson State Community College
EDWARD E. PENHOET, Chiron Corporation
JAMES W. SERUM, Hewlett-Packard Company
ELAINE SEYMOUR, University of Colorado, Boulder
CHRISTY VOGEL, Cabrillo College
DAVID WILKINSON (NAS*), Princeton University

Former members†

C. BRADLEY MOORE (NAS*), University of California, Berkeley, *Past Chair*
ISAAC ABELLA, University of Chicago
NEAL ABRAHAM, De Pauw University
GEORGE R. BOGGS, Palomar College
DENICE D. DENTON, University of Washington
MICHAEL P. DOYLE, Research Corporation
RAMESH GANGOLLI, University of Washington
FREDERICK T. GRAYBEAL, ASARCO Incorporated
NORMAN HACKERMAN (NAS*), The Robert A. Welch Foundation
JOHN K. HAYNES, Morehouse College
EILEEN DELGADO JOHANN, Miami-Dade Community College
WILLIAM E. KIRWAN, Ohio State University
SHARON LONG (NAS*), Stanford University
DOROTHY MERRITTS, Franklin and Marshall College
JOHN A. MOORE (NAS*), University of California at Riverside
PENNY MOORE, Piedmont High School
W. ANN REYNOLDS, University of Alabama at Birmingham

*NAS: Member of the National Academy of Sciences
†These former members of CUSE participated in the development of this report and have approved its contents.

REVIEWERS

This report has been reviewed in draft form by individuals chosen for their diverse perspectives and technical expertise, in accordance with procedures approved by the National Research Council's (NRC's) Report Review Committee. The purpose of this independent review is to provide candid and critical comments that will assist the institution in making the published report as sound as possible and to ensure that the report meets institutional standards for objectivity, evidence, and responsiveness to the study charge. The review comments and draft manuscript remain confidential to protect the integrity of the deliberative process. We wish to thank the following individuals for their participation in the review of this report:

THEODORE BELYTSCHKO (NAE*), Northwestern University
JOHN BOLLINGER (NAE*), University of Wisconsin, Madison
BONNIE BRUNKHORST, California State University, San Bernadino
WILLIAM DANFORTH (IOM*), Washington University
JAMES DUDERSTADT (NAE*), University of Michigan, Ann Arbor
JOAN GIRGUS, Princeton University
DAVID KAUFFMAN, University of New Mexico
JERRY MOHRIG, Carleton College
NORMAN NESS (NAS*), University of Delaware
RONALD RUSAY, Diablo Valley College
BRUCE SHERWOOD, Carnegie Mellon University
BROCK SPENCER, Beloit College
JAMES STITH, American Institute of Physics
SAMUEL WARD, University of Arizona

While the individuals listed above have provided many constructive comments and suggestions, responsibility for the final content of this report rests solely with the authoring committee and the National Research Council.

*NAS: Member of the National Academy of Sciences; NAE: Member of the National Academy of Engineering; IOM: Member of the Institute of Medicine

STAFF

JAY B. LABOV, Study Director
Center for Science, Mathematics, and Engineering Education

NANCY L. DEVINO, Senior Staff Officer
Center for Science, Mathematics, and Engineering Education

KATHLEEN (KIT) JOHNSTON, Senior Editor
Center for Science, Mathematics, and Engineering Education

GAIL E. PRITCHARD, Research Associate
Center for Science, Mathematics, and Engineering Education

TERRY K. HOLMER, Senior Project Assistant
Center for Science, Mathematics, and Engineering Education

TABLE OF CONTENTS

FOREWORD

A CALL TO ACTION

What does it mean to be scientifically, mathematically, and technologically literate in our society? When and how do young people begin to develop the requisite skills and knowledge, and what is the responsibility of the scientific community in helping them do so? Early childhood studies about how and at what developmental stages children learn various kinds of information and concepts are helping us to understand the kinds of intervention and education that are important well before formal schooling begins. The consensus visions of national standards in science, mathematics, and technology are helping us to develop learning goals in these subjects for students in grades K-12. As these goals become realized, we must maintain incentives for students to build and expand on their experiences through their undergraduate years. We must do this for all students, both those who do and those who do not aspire to be scientists, mathematicians, and engineers.

Many recent reports calling for reform in the education of undergraduates in the United States indicate that the faculty and administrative leaders of our nation's postsecondary institutions and those who work with or advise them have much work to do. For example, *From Analysis to Action: Undergraduate Education in Science, Mathematics, Engineering, and Technology* (National Research Council, 1996a) reported that "from some of the most prestigious institutions . . . it is possible for students to graduate with not more than six percent of their work in the sciences and technology." *Shaping the Future: New Expectations for Undergraduate Education in Science, Mathematics, Engineering, and Technology*

(National Science Foundation, 1996b) reviewed ". . .the needs of all undergraduates attending all types of U.S. two-and four-year colleges and universities" and concluded that the goal must be, "All students have access to supportive, excellent undergraduate education in science, mathematics, engineering, and technology, and all students learn these subjects by direct experience with the methods and processes of inquiry."

The National Research Council's (NRC) Committee on Undergraduate Education (CUSE) used these two reports as a basis for discussion and debate during a "Year of Dialogue" with hundreds of representatives from a broad cross section of the nation's pre-college and postsecondary institutions. Participants included chief academic officers, department chairs, and individual faculty from two- and four-year colleges and universities as well as school administrators and faculty from K-12 institutions. These diverse stakeholders in science, mathematics, engineering, and technology (SME&T) education agreed that specific visions of change and specific strategies for taking action were needed to help move forward the reform of undergraduate SME&T education. In this, the ensuing report, six such visions and attendant recommendations are provided. They pinpoint key changes that all postsecondary institutions, from research universities to community colleges, must undertake if they wish to provide all undergraduates—including our current and future K-12 and postsecondary teachers—with a high-quality SME&T education.

Particularly powerful aspects of this report include its primary goal, which proposes that all institutions of higher education provide

". . . diverse opportunities for all undergraduates to study science, mathematics, engineering, and technology as practiced by scientists and engineers, and as early in their academic careers as possible." In addition, the authoring committee has taken great care to address both the separate and complementary roles that various members of the campus community could play in realizing this goal. Chief academic officers, so often unacknowledged as key stakeholders in changes of this magnitude, are encouraged to assume a primary leadership role. Important, as well, are the specific strategies provided in the report to help chief academic officers, individual faculty, and academic departments improve all aspects of undergraduate SME&T education. These strategies include raising expectations for pre-college preparation in SME&T, providing inquiry-based and interdisciplinary approaches to teaching and learning (especially in the early undergraduate years), evaluating courses in ways that measure student learning, strengthening institutions' academic and administrative infrastructures, and better preparing future teachers of pre-college and undergraduate students.

This report also clearly articulates the *joint* roles and responsibilities of faculty and administrators in schools of education and in schools of arts and sciences to develop much more well-integrated programs to educate current and future teachers of K-12 mathematics and science. Specific recommendations contain extensive references to the scholarly literature on this subject. Also included are descriptions of institutions and programs that are taking steps to provide students with the participatory education in science, mathematics, and technology that is called for in this report.

Like the authors of the previous reports, the members of CUSE recognize that consensus does not yet exist in the postsecondary community about how to address the many problems facing SME&T education or the broader issue of scientific literacy for all. However, as participants in the "Year of Dialogue" amply demonstrated, there is much agreement about the barriers that hinder improvements in undergraduate education and what must be done to overcome them.

This acknowledgment of issues from within academe, coupled with increasing external demands that colleges and universities devote more attention and resources to educating the nation's undergraduates effectively, indicate that now is the time for the higher education community to act decisively. *Transforming Undergraduate Education in Science, Mathematics, Engineering, and Technology* suggests a series of blueprints for doing so. With a firm commitment to changing undergraduate SME&T education by *all* stakeholders in higher education, undergraduate students, schoolchildren (whose scientific literacy depends upon how higher education prepares teachers for our nation's classrooms), and the public at-large all will be prepared to understand, appreciate, and take advantage of challenges that science and technology provide in the future.

Bruce M. Alberts, President
National Academy of Sciences

PREFACE

In 1993, the National Research Council (NRC) established the Committee on Undergraduate Science Education (CUSE) as a joint initiative of the Commission on Physical Sciences, Mathematics, and Applications and the Commission on Life Sciences. This standing committee is now an integral component of the NRC's Center for Science, Mathematics, and Engineering Education.

Charged by the NRC with seeking ways to improve scientific literacy for all undergraduates, the committee has worked to identify, develop, and promote implementation of undergraduate programs that enrich the understanding and appreciation of scientific knowledge and improve the skills necessary for continued learning, productive lives, and informed decision making.

To date, the committee has published two reports, entitled *Science Teaching Reconsidered: A Handbook* (National Research Council, 1997a) and *Science Teacher Preparation in an Era of Standards-Based Reform* (National Research Council, 1997b). The committee also provided comments on the *National Science Education Standards* (National Research Council, 1996b). These reports are available free of charge on the World Wide Web at <http://www.nap.edu> In addition, a short introduction to the *National Science Education Standards* has been provided as an appendix to this report (see Appendix D).

In late 1995, the committee embarked on the work that would directly lead to the publication of *Transforming Undergraduate Education in Science, Mathematics, Engineering, and Technology*. Through the generous support of the Exxon Education Foundation, the committee hosted a series of regional symposia and topical forums—a "Year of

Dialogue"—to explore many of the issues raised by the NRC and National Science Foundation reports on undergraduate education respectively entitled *From Analysis to Action: Undergraduate Education in Science, Mathematics, Engineering, and Technology* (National Research Council, 1996a) and *Shaping the Future: New Expectations for Undergraduate Education in Science, Mathematics, Engineering, and Technology* (National Science Foundation, 1996b). These reports are also available free of charge on the World Wide Web at <http://www.nap.edu>

This report's primary goal, six vision statements, and multiple strategies for implementing the visions are designed to assist top-level academic officers, individual faculty, and departments in the critical process of institutionalizing the improvement of undergraduate science, mathematics, engineering, and technology (SME&T) education. The content of the report was informed by and reflects the "Year of Dialogue," which is detailed in Appendix A. It also reflects research findings on undergraduate SME&T education and many discussions held before and since the "Year of Dialogue" with national organizations for science, mathematics, engineering, and technology education and with faculty and chief academic officers from a variety of institutions of higher education across the country.

Transforming Undergraduate Education in Science, Mathematics, Engineering, and Technology is written to encourage members of the postsecondary SME&T community to reflect on the following kinds of questions related to undergraduate education (modified from Fox, 1998):

Science education for *all* undergraduates: Are we exposing all of our students to the kinds of effective teaching techniques and meaningful educational experiences that truly excite them about SME&T? Do we actively engage students in SME&T in ways similar to how we work as scientists, mathematicians, or engineers, given that the vast majority of students in our introductory courses will never again have formal exposure to our disciplines? Are we providing students with the intellectual skills and background they will need to appreciate and continue learning about SME&T throughout their lives? Are we helping our students understand "real world" applications of SME&T? Do we make explicit connections between our disciplines and others in the natural sciences, social sciences, and the humanities in our courses and when advising students?

Preparation of future K-12 and undergraduate teachers of science, mathematics, and technology: Are we preparing future teachers to engage the next generation of students in science, mathematics, and technology? Do we, as undergraduate faculty, model the kind of teaching and promote the kind of learning we would like to see in grades K-12? Do we encourage our graduate students and post-doctoral fellows to think seriously about quality teaching of undergraduates both in their current roles as teaching assistants and in their future roles as faculty members?

Retention of SME&T majors: Seymour and Hewitt (1997) have carefully documented the distressingly high numbers of students who enter college with intentions of pursuing majors in SME&T and then change paths shortly thereafter. Are we doing enough to encourage these students to continue their study of SME&T by engaging their interests while they are enrolled in our introductory courses? In addition to the rigorous disciplinary content contained within introductory courses for prospective majors, do these courses also provide students with connections to broad SME&T concepts, including applications to the natural and engineered worlds? Do we work with colleagues in other SME&T departments to integrate information and concepts from other required courses into our own courses? Do upper-division courses build upon rather than repeat concepts that students learned in their introductory SME&T courses? Are our curricula structured to offer "gateways" in their later undergraduate years to students who did not pursue SME&T majors in their first year? Do we, as faculty, know enough about the myriad career opportunities that are available to SME&T majors to advise them properly?

Making teaching community property (Shulman, 1993): Do we speak with departmental colleagues often enough (or at all?) about pedagogy and curriculum or how we present and integrate concepts in our lower- and upper-division courses? Have we, as departments or institutions, articulated what we want our students to know and be able to do in SME&T by the time they complete their formal studies with us, either at the introductory or advanced levels? Do our institutions encourage and provide support for faculty to attend professional meetings where they can both disseminate and learn about new ideas for improving undergraduate SME&T education? Do our institutions and their leaders also encourage, recognize, and appropriately reward departments and other program units that undertake a serious examination of their curricular offerings and strive to introduce effective, innovative approaches to teaching and learning in their courses?

Obligations of the disciplines: Do the professional societies to which we belong devote sufficient attention and resources to improving undergraduate education? Do these organizations encourage their members to participate in education projects and activities at meetings or through other venues? Do they publicly recognize members who have demonstrated excellence and innovation in teaching, both within their disciplines and in related interdisciplinary areas? Do they assist members in improving their teaching by providing pedagogical materials or access to such resources through society publications or websites? Do they provide opportunities for members to publish peer-reviewed papers on innovations in teaching and learning in their professional journals?

As our committee continues to work toward its goals, we will interact extensively with colleagues in the higher education and the K-12 communities. We welcome your comments and suggestions about how we can be most effective in working with the SME&T community to promote change.

Marye Anne Fox, Chair
Committee on Undergraduate
Science Education

EXECUTIVE SUMMARY

Through science, mathematics, and engineering, our nation continues to lead the world in the development and utilization of new technologies. Whether related to our health, to the environment, or to our production and use of material goods, science, mathematics, engineering, and technology (SME&T) are integral and essential parts of daily life for virtually everyone in the United States and around the globe. However, the understanding of SME&T by most Americans, which reflects the level of SME&T education most Americans have had, is inadequate for full participation in this increasingly technological world. Our nation is becoming divided into a technologically knowledgeable elite and a disadvantaged majority. Given the large and increasing numbers of students in the higher education system and the fact that all teachers of grades K-12 are products of that system, improving SME&T education, particularly at the undergraduate level, could be a critical means for closing the gap.

Changes are needed in current approaches to teaching SME&T at the undergraduate level as well as in graduate training and continuing education for teachers. To effect these changes is an enormous challenge. However, on campuses across the United States, many individuals are making substantive improvements to SME&T courses, programs, and curricula. The time has now come for the institutionalization and sharing of these improvements. Nothing less than the fundamental reform of American postsecondary SME&T education is at stake.

To guide the institutionalization and sharing of postsecondary SME&T education reform, primarily at the undergraduate level, the authoring committee of this report—the

Committee on Undergraduate Science Education (CUSE)—has adopted a **primary goal**. It is based on five years of research and discussions with members of many sectors of the higher education SME&T community, including two years of intensive research into and consultations about major issues in SME&T undergraduate education.

Institutions of higher education should provide diverse opportunities for *all* undergraduates to study science, mathematics, engineering, and technology as practiced by scientists and engineers, and as early in their academic careers as possible.

This fundamental goal informs all that follows in this report. It embraces and builds upon the educational imperatives stated in the National Research Council report entitled *From Analysis to Action: Undergraduate Education in Science, Mathematics, Engineering, and Technology* (1996a), the National Science Foundation Advisory Committee's report entitled *Shaping the Future: New Expectations for Undergraduate Education in Science, Mathematics, Engineering, and Technology* (1996b), and the Boyer Commission's report entitled *Reinventing Undergraduate Education: A Blueprint for America's Research Universities* (1998). It requires that the improvement of undergraduate SME&T education begin with a reexamination and restructuring of introductory and lower-level courses and programs. It is meant to benefit both those students who will go on to careers as professional scientists, mathematicians, engineers, or teachers for grades K-12, as well as the vast majority of undergraduate students who do not plan to declare SME&T or education majors. It provides strategies for implementation that are appropriate for the range of two- and four-year postsecondary institutions in this country.

Readers will note that while this report, its visions, and many of its strategies address the breadth of undergraduate SME&T education, many of the report's examples of innovative practice are drawn from undergraduate science education. The committee would like to state here that many of the issues being debated in science education also apply to mathematics, engineering, and technology education. For example, the issues and recommendations addressed in *Engineering Education: Designing an Adaptive System* (National Research Council, 1995a) are quite congruent with the issues and visions of this report. In addition, many of the federal agencies that support science education (e.g., the National Science Foundation) are calling for greater integration among the disciplines. This report addresses the larger SME&T community in that spirit, as well.

The committee acknowledges that achievement of the primary goal in the context of lasting reform will require execution of an exceedingly complex array of tasks by virtually all academic and service components of a college or university. This will require the commitment of faculty, academic administrators, academic support units (e.g., campus teaching and learning centers), facility planners, and undergraduate and graduate students. The organizational structure—and even the priorities of missions of many postsecondary institutions—will be fundamentally challenged. Therefore, committee members conclude that **top officials in colleges and universities will need to play a special role**: they will need to exert strong leadership, to display a deep understanding of the issues, and to provide tangible support for the necessary changes to take hold.

The committee also recognizes that implementing the visions of this report will require new funds or shifts in the allocation of

resources. Costs may vary considerably from institution to institution. With the evidence and information provided in this report, the committee hopes to stimulate serious discussions at all higher education institutions that will take into account the need for new or reallocated resources to implement change.

What follows the statement of the primary goal, both here and in the body of the report, is a series of vision statements to which all postsecondary institutions might aspire. Extensive background and references support each vision statement, brief synopses of which are given below. Specific implementation strategies for improving many aspects of science education also accompany each vision, details of which are provided in the body of the report. These strategies for implementation indicate what chief academic officers, faculty members, and academic departments can do individually and collectively to improve undergraduate science education, and by so doing, ensure that many more citizens can become full participants in our nation's scientific and technological future.

VISION 1

All postsecondary institutions would require all entering students to undertake college-level studies in SME&T. Entry into higher education would include assessment of students' understanding of these subjects that is based on the recommendations of national K-12 standards.

If undergraduates are to view SME&T as an integral component of their education, the stage should be set long before they enter college. Ideally, their pre-college experience should have included both quality instruction in standards-based classrooms and a clear awareness that achievement in science, mathematics, and technology will be expected for admission to college. Once implemented,

Strategies for Promoting and Implementing Vision 1

Executive and academic officers of postsecondary institutions can implement Vision 1 by	*Individual faculty and academic departments can implement Vision 1 by*
1. Asking academic SME&T departments and the Office of Admissions to establish appropriate institutional admissions standards for science and mathematics preparation.	1. Responding to both the current educational experiences and accomplishments of today's students and to the changing expectations about what pre-college students should know and should be able to do in SME&T as a result of the increased use of national and statewide standards-based curricula and assessment tools. 2. Working with their institution's Office of Admissions to make clear to prospective students the departments' expectations for entry into SME&T programs and the institution's goal of providing SME&T education to all of its enrolled students.

standards-based approaches to science and mathematics (and eventually technology) education should enable more students to reach these desired levels of achievement.

However, the committee recognizes that standards-based K-12 education in science, mathematics, and technology is not yet available to most students across the country. Colleges and universities must now rely on standardized examinations in these disciplines that do not necessarily assess the kinds of learning emphasized in national standards. Many postsecondary institutions also employ open admission policies. Such policies provide critical educational opportunities for students who may not have had the academic experiences called for by national and state standards.

Moving K-12 education to a system that is more consonant with standards will likely require at least a decade. Nevertheless, change is occurring—albeit at different rates—in many parts of the country, and increasing numbers of students are likely to arrive at postsecondary institutions with greater exposure to science and mathematics standards. Thus, postsecondary institutions, their admissions offices, and faculty will need to monitor these trends in K-12 education

with respect to admissions policies and the content and teaching of undergraduate courses. Admissions policies should be revisited regularly to account for changes taking place in the K-12 sector.

The committee also recognizes that, although this vision and the accompanying implementation strategies are appropriate for a majority of students in the nation's high schools, many other students will need creative alternative pathways to higher education. These students include those who have not performed well academically in high school but who have potential to succeed at college-level studies and those who did not receive the kind of education articulated in this report and who, as adults, are now seeking additional education.

VISION 2

SME&T would become an integral part of the curriculum for all undergraduate students through required introductory courses that engage all students in SME&T and their connections to society and the human condition.

Science is an integral part of our daily lives. It also is an historical and procedural foundation for human thinking about and understanding of the natural and engineered worlds. Therefore, colleges and universities should require that *all* entering students, irrespective of their ultimate selection of a major, undertake college-level studies in SME&T. Science majors would gain a focused, in-depth exposure to scientific principles, and those who wished to do so could build on these experiences to participate in faculty-supervised original research. They and all non-science students would also enroll in courses that focus on providing awareness, understanding, and appreciation of the natural and human-constructed worlds and that involve at least one laboratory experience. Introductory undergraduate curricula would incorporate physical, biological, and mathematical sciences, engineering, and technology in a manner that allowed all students to understand and appreciate the interrelationships among these disciplines in the context of human society. All of these courses would include topics that are both intellectually challenging and near the frontiers of inquiry. Wherever possible, these topics would engage students in discussing problems that students would find timely and important.

If this vision were to be realized, faculty would design and offer introductory science courses that met the needs of students with diverse educational backgrounds, experiences, interests, aspirations, and learning styles. These courses would be high-quality, laboratory-rich experiences that are meaningful and appropriate for all undergraduate students regardless of their intended majors. In addition to presenting content information in one or more areas of science, these courses would engage undergraduates in exploring the fundamental and unifying concepts and processes of science. They would be interdisciplinary in nature and focus, providing case studies that examine real problems and applications. They would emphasize the evolving

processes of scientific thought and inquiry and would encourage and assist students to understand the need to be lifelong learners of SME&T. In short, these lower-division courses would be designed in content and subject matter approach in such a way as to encourage many students to continue to advance, rather than to end, their SME&T study. That is, the courses would serve as "pumps" to, rather than "filters" out of, higher levels of study in SME&T.

The creation and support of innovative courses also would include the building of a sophisticated communications infrastructure so that students, faculty, and local, state, national, and international communities could share ideas, strategies, and solutions for richer, more genuine educational experiences. Collectively, this communications network (constructed primarily on the Internet) would deepen the reform of undergraduate SME&T courses. An important contribution would be the effective use of information technologies in SME&T curricula.[1]

In addition, *all* programs in SME&T would be structured to allow as many undergraduate students as possible to engage in original, supervised research under the tutelage of a faculty or senior graduate student mentor. Undergraduates would become involved with as many phases of a research project as time permitted. These might include experimental design, searching the literature, performing the research using modern scientific instruments and techniques, analyzing and interpreting data, and preparing a report for publication or presentation at an institutional, regional, or national scientific meeting. SME&T majors would undertake such research for a minimum of one academic term, although research experiences that last for longer periods of time would be

[1]The NRC's Committee on Information Technology, under the auspices of the Center for Science, Mathematics, and Engineering Education, anticipates concluding by the spring of 1999 a study on effective, appropriate use of information technology to enhance SME&T courses. More information on this project can be found at the National Academy of Sciences' home page, <http://www.nas.edu>, under "Current Projects."

Strategies for Promoting and Implementing Vision 2

Executive and academic officers of postsecondary institutions can implement Vision 2 by

1. At institutions with active research programs, convening a local blue-ribbon panel of faculty who are recognized for their contributions to both research and teaching to report on what is needed to offer a cutting-edge SME&T curriculum for undergraduates on their campuses consistent with their institutions' respective missions.
2. Supporting the inclusion of core SME&T requirements and core course offerings that include at least one or preferably more laboratory experiences at the undergraduate level for all students and an option for independent research for all science majors.
3. Encouraging individual faculty to learn to develop new and innovative courses and make existing courses more effective by promoting an institutional culture that rewards this participation and that provides technical support.
4. Providing incentives for individual faculty and departments in SME&T, the humanities, and the social sciences to work together to develop introductory interdisciplinary courses that are meaningful for *all* students, including both those who are and who are not likely to major in the faculty members' disciplines.
5. Encouraging senior SME&T faculty who have been recognized for teaching excellence and innovation to participate in lower-division course offerings and in curriculum planning.
6. Establishing reward incentives for faculty and departments to contribute to the sustained availability of interdepartmental, integrative courses and excellence in teaching.
7. Providing avenues for students, alumni, professional advisory groups, and the community to participate in the development of new, interdisciplinary courses.
8. Encouraging faculty to interact with partners both across campus and at other nearby two- and four-year institutions in order to share effective teaching practices and course and curricular innovations.
9. Including the space needs of lower-division teaching in active learning environments and of undergraduate research participation when planning for capital improvement projects and allocating resources.

Individual faculty and academic departments can implement Vision 2 by

1. Working with colleagues who teach introductory interdisciplinary courses to delineate carefully fundamental concepts about the natural and human-constructed worlds to which students should be exposed.
2. Devising a plan for involving all undergraduates in at least one laboratory experience, including—for all interested SME&T majors—an experience in supervised original research on- or off-campus for at least one academic term.
3. Emphasizing the development of introductory SME&T courses that include applications and hands-on learning experiences.
4. Sharing course syllabi, examinations, assignments, and laboratory experiments, expectations, successes, and failures with departmental colleagues, other faculty members, and academic advisors whose students are taking innovative, introductory SME&T courses.
5. Adopting formal mechanisms whereby faculty in different departments who teach similar concepts can share information about what is being learned in innovative courses, including the use of effective techniques and materials.
6. Encouraging faculty who were not original designers of an innovation to participate in the resulting courses without having to take full responsibility for teaching or maintaining them.
7. Discussing curricular as well as non-curricular issues (e.g., use and sharing of facilities and equipment) with everyone involved with an interdisciplinary course.
8. Offering local workshops, possibly seeking the advice of outside experts from other two- and four-year institutions, on innovations that foster undergraduate learning.

encouraged whenever possible. Other students, especially those who aspire to careers in teaching, would be encouraged to participate in original research, either through inquiry-based laboratory experiences associated with SME&T courses or through the kinds of supervised research opportunities available to SME&T majors. For research experiences lasting one semester or less, students might become involved with faculty- or student-originated projects in progress or with smaller projects designed by a faculty member and a group of students in a research-based course.

VISION 3

All colleges and universities would continually and systematically evaluate the efficacy of courses in SME&T.

Faculty would continually evaluate their courses for efficacy in promoting student learning. Such evaluations would reflect in part the emphases outlined for **Vision 2**. Thus, in addition to mastery of the specific subject matter taught in a course, success would be defined and measured by the degree of understanding and appreciation gained by students of both general scientific concepts and of the scientific approach to understanding natural processes. Evaluations would include measurements of learning at several levels: in the courses themselves, in subsequent SME&T courses, and, ultimately, in career and life. The results of such evaluations would be used continually to produce improvements in courses for students both inside and outside of the major, to assist in the professional development of individual faculty, and to allow departments continually to assess and improve their curricular offerings.

Strategies for Promoting and Implementing Vision 3

Executive and academic officers of postsecondary institutions can implement Vision 3 by

1. Benchmarking undergraduate programs within their institutions against the best practices of peer institutions.

2. Requiring that any proposal submitted to the institution that seeks funds to create new courses, to modify existing courses, or to explore some alternative approach to teaching SME&T courses contain information about how the course or teaching practice will be evaluated for effectiveness.

3. Encouraging participation in departmental assessments as a significant component of individual faculty evaluations for promotion, tenure, and post-tenure review.

Individual faculty and academic departments can implement Vision 3 by

1. Setting clear learning goals for individual courses and for the department's curriculum in general, especially for introductory and general education courses that the department oversees.

2. Including both undergraduate and graduate student representatives in departmental discussions about individual courses and/or curricular issues.

3. Involving departmental colleagues in substantive, regular evaluation of teaching and curriculum.

4. Providing active learning environments for all students, even in large section, lecture-dominated courses.

5. Hiring within SME&T departments individuals who wish to pursue research on how undergraduate students learn.

VISION 4

SME&T faculties would assume greater responsibility for the pre-service and in-service education of K-12 teachers.

Improving the SME&T education of both pre-service and in-service K-12 teachers is one of the most important challenges facing college and university faculties.[2] Scientists, mathematicians, engineers, and teacher educators all need to share responsibility for teacher preparation (e.g., Riley, 1998). If **Vision 4** were to be realized, these faculty would provide integrated pre-service and in-service experiences that blend scientific knowledge with pedagogical methods and effective teaching practices. Teacher education programs would be informed by the *National Science Education Standards* (National Research Council, 1996b), the *Curriculum and Evaluation Standards for School Mathematics* and the *Professional Development Standards for Teaching Mathematics* (National Council of Teachers of Mathematics, 1989, 1991), the *Standards for Technology Education* (The International Technology Education Association, in preparation[3]), and other national and state-level science and mathematics education reform initiatives (e.g., American Association for the Advancement of Science, 1993; Council of Chief State School Officers, 1997).

A critical component of new teacher preparation programs would be the adoption of teaching approaches that enhance pre-service teachers' desire to continue both their professional development and their own personal learning. SME&T faculty need to become involved in this effort by providing motivating pre-service and in-service opportunities

---

Strategies for Promoting and Implementing Vision 4

Executive and academic officers of postsecondary institutions can implement Vision 4 by

1. Making available new tenure-track faculty positions for candidates with dual backgrounds in a SME&T discipline and in science education who are interested in promoting innovative and effective undergraduate learning.

2. Actively promoting partnerships, consortia, or outreach programs with local school districts to advance the professional development of teachers and to provide resources not otherwise available to local schools.

3. Removing institutional obstacles to department donations and continued servicing of high-quality equipment to local school districts.

Individual faculty and academic departments can implement Vision 4 by

1. Measuring the effectiveness of each component of the pre-service curriculum in fostering innovative and effective pedagogy and in exploring SME&T concepts.

2. Inviting regional K-12 science and mathematics teachers to participate in on-campus seminars where recent scientific or pedagogical research is discussed.

3. Inviting master teachers to serve as adjunct faculty and colleagues in **both** schools of education and SME&T departments.

---

[2]For a more in-depth study of this topic, see the National Commission on Teaching and America's Future reports, *What Matters Most: Teaching for America's Future* (National Commission on Teaching and America's Future, 1996), and *Doing What Matters Most: Investing in Quality Teaching* (Darling-Hammond, 1997), which explain the challenges of preparing future teachers and offer findings and recommendations for improvement.

[3]The *Standards for Technology Education* are expected to be released in early spring of 1999. CUSE members have not reviewed the standards but know that the authoring committee, the International Technology Education Association (ITEA), has modeled its efforts on the standards work of the National Council of Teachers of Mathematics and the National Research Council. Indeed, several members of these earlier standards efforts are members of the ITEA working group.

Executive and academic officers of postsecondary institutions can implement Vision 4 by

4. Establishing an institutional "hot line" telephone number or current events website to provide local teachers with information about departmental or campus-wide events involving SME&T speakers or other activities.

5. Providing incentives for faculty from schools of education and SME&T departments to work together to develop both certification options for science majors and continuing education courses for teachers that specifically examine the NCTM's *Professional Standards for Teaching Mathematics* and *Curriculum and Evaluation Standards for School Mathematics*, the *National Science Education Standards, Benchmarks for Science Literacy, Standards for Technology Education* (in preparation), and state curriculum frameworks and how these can be implemented at various grade levels.

6. Making available financial resources to hire local master teachers as adjunct faculty to work with faculty in both schools of education and SME&T departments on improving pre-service education and in assessing student learning.

Individual faculty and academic departments can implement Vision 4 by

4. Employing discipline-based science teachers in the continuing education of fellow teachers.

for scientific discovery for K-12 science educators in the classroom, in laboratories, and in the field. Pre-service opportunities also could include classroom teachers and scientists working together with students through school/college partnerships.

VISION 5

All postsecondary institutions would provide the rewards and recognition, resources, tools, and infrastructure necessary to promote innovative and effective undergraduate SME&T teaching and learning.

The central importance of offering high-quality introductory SME&T courses must be visibly recognized through appropriate recognition of and rewards to individual faculty and staff and, collectively, to departmental and other program units. If **Vision 5** were to be realized, postsecondary institutions would recognize and appropriately reward faculty leaders and departments or program units that have introduced new teaching and learning methods into their courses and curricular programs. Modern tools (e.g., access to information technology) and other kinds of institutional support would be provided to faculty and staff who wanted to use these tools in their classrooms and laboratories. Well-staffed resource centers would be provided where faculty and students could obtain the latest information about alternative and effective teaching and learning techniques. These resource centers also would serve as sites for piloting new programs and practicing effective teaching and assessment activities.

The authoring committee recognizes that implementing the visions of this report could require new funds or shifts in the allocation of resources. The costs involved may vary considerably from institution to institution. With the evidence and information provided in this report, the committee hopes to stimulate serious discussions at all higher education institutions that will take into account the need for new or reallocated resources to implement change.

Strategies for Promoting and Implementing Vision 5

Executive and academic officers of postsecondary institutions can implement Vision 5 by

1. Creating both general and discipline-based Teaching and Learning Centers that
   - provide advice and technical support so that innovations can be implemented successfully;
   - provide students with internships, assistantships, or fellowships to encourage input into the development of courses; and
   - offer small grants to provide faculty with released time or other resources for particularly innovative SME&T course development that exceeds substantially the normal course preparation commitment.

2. Providing incentives, including recognition, to individual faculty to upgrade their teaching skills and knowledge of educational issues by participating in programs at their institution's Teaching and Learning Center and in departmental or cross-disciplinary seminars and workshops.

3. Providing incentives, including institutional recognition and additional financial support, to departments and other program units that collectively work to improve teaching, student learning, and curricular offerings to meet the needs of *all* of their students.

4. Making easily accessible to the faculty new software useful for common tasks, including those associated with innovative SME&T courses.

5. Devising a comprehensive plan to update or replace computer hardware, software, and associated resources on a regular basis.

6. Working to assess and meet institution-wide needs for space, equipment, and other resources needed to upgrade and improve the curriculum.

Individual faculty and academic departments can implement Vision 5 by

1. Including a scholarly assessment of faculty participation in improving teaching and curriculum as one of the criteria for promotion, tenure, and other personnel decisions.

2. Using a departmental vision and plan for curricular innovation to guide requests for space and/or facilities utilization.

3. Allocating space for students to work together in environments equipped with readily accessible visualization and computational tools.

4. Discussing case studies of innovative and effective practices in science and mathematics teaching as a routine part of departmental business.

5. Discussing with colleagues information about effective teaching practices that is increasingly available on the World Wide Web.

VISION 6

Postsecondary institutions would provide quality experiences that encourage graduate and postdoctoral students, and especially those who aspire to careers as postsecondary faculty in SME&T disciplines, to become skilled teachers and current postsecondary faculty to acquire additional knowledge about how teaching methods affect student learning.

Graduate degree programs should provide graduate and postdoctoral students with training in the pedagogical skills they need to teach undergraduates effectively in classroom, laboratory, and field settings. In adopting **Vision 6**, universities also would provide all faculty with resources and opportunities for continuing professional development, informal education, and professional interaction with their higher education colleagues to help faculty enhance their professional skills and expertise as teacher-scholars throughout their academic careers.

The committee recognizes that not all of the recommendations and strategies for implementation provided above and in the main body of the report will be equally useful or applicable to all postsecondary institutions. Different institutional histories, patterns of governance, campus cultures, and efforts to date to improve undergraduate education may make some implementation strategies more useful than others for a given institution. For example, many of the strategies for implementing **Vision 6** (changes in graduate and postdoctoral programs) will not apply to community colleges and four-year undergraduate institutions. However, the committee believes that most SME&T departments and institutions should be able to utilize or adopt many of the implementation strategies offered in the report. The committee also recommends that all SME&T programs at two- and four-year colleges and universities work with other professional schools on campus that have direct or indirect interests in SME&T education (e.g., education, medical, business, and law schools), with programs in the humanities and social sciences, and with SME&T departments at other institutions in their regions.

Strategies for Promoting and Implementing Vision 6

Executive and academic officers of postsecondary institutions can implement Vision 6 by

1. Working with graduate faculties to establish programs that integrate discussion of important current issues in teaching and learning while both faculty and graduate teaching assistants acquire new teaching skills.

2. Establishing arrangements with community colleges, other undergraduate institutions, and K-12 schools that allow graduate and postdoctoral students to experience teaching at these types of schools.

3. Providing infrastructure that encourages graduate student and faculty access to publications, videos, and other materials that address the improvement of undergraduate teaching.

4. Encouraging appropriate academic departments and campus service units to assist graduates with preparing summaries of their work in a form accessible to the general public.

Individual faculty and academic departments can implement Vision 6 by

1. Encouraging departments to offer graduate and postdoctoral students opportunities to improve their teaching skills in laboratories, classrooms, and in the field, even when such activities might compete with time dedicated to individual research.

2. Serving as role models and mentors for graduate and postdoctoral students interested in pursuing careers in K-12 or postsecondary teaching.

3. Asking invited speakers at departmental colloquia to discuss briefly aspects of their teaching as a routine part of the introduction to their scientific work or educational research.

4. Reserving time at department meetings to discuss participation of graduate students in curriculum, assessment, and other educational issues.

5. As part of the interview process, asking faculty candidates to present a general lecture to undergraduates on a topic selected by the department or program or to give a pedagogical seminar to faculty and graduate students that discusses some aspect of teaching.

INTRODUCTION

As a nation, the United States is creating opportunities and challenges for the future that may be unparalleled in recorded human history. However, as was heralded in a publication some 15 years ago (National Commission on Excellence in Education. 1983) and as indicated by the results of the Third International Mathematics and Science Study (TIMSS), educationally we are still very much a nation at risk (Pister and Rowe, 1993; National Research Council, 1997e; National Assessment of Educational Progress, 1997; U.S. Department of Education, 1998a).

During the years immediately following the launch of Sputnik, the United States overhauled its educational system to encourage the training of science and engineering specialists needed to meet the technological and military challenges presented by the Soviet Union. In succeeding years, our nation has defined the leading edge for most scientific and technical fields, and advancements in these fields have played an ever-increasing role in the life of our nation and its citizens.

As has been well documented, the scientific literacy of most Americans has not kept pace with the central role that science and technology play in their personal lives or in their communities. Indeed, to be effective in tomorrow's society, people will need to be able to think more analytically about events, objects, and processes and to analyze them in the context of natural phenomena (e.g., Rutherford and Ahlgren, 1990; National Education Goals Panel, 1997).

National and state standards-based reforms in grades K-12 across the country have the potential to change fundamentally the ways in which all primary and secondary students learn science and mathematics. While this potential has not yet been realized uniformly, increasing numbers of pre-college students are learning through reform-based teaching and methods. Increasingly, college

---

"If the United States is to ensure a competitive workforce which possesses the necessary scientific and technological skills to fill the jobs of the future and compete in a global economy, we must develop the mathematics and science skills of all of our students, not simply the very best."

National Education Goals Panel, 1997, pg. 9

---

and university faculty find that they are being challenged to guide the postsecondary SME&T education of students with heterogeneous experiences and interests. For several important reasons, change in lower-division undergraduate education is key:

- **Lower-division undergraduate science and mathematics education prepares a large proportion of the nation's leaders.** Most of our nation's leaders—policy- and decision-makers—matriculate at institutions of higher education. Because most of them do not pursue formal career tracks in science, mathematics, or engineering, the undergraduate years are the last time that they—and most other undergraduate students—are asked to think broadly about SME&T in any formal way. Nonetheless, these graduates will go on to have an impact on scientific research, technological advances, and the resolution of technologically related issues through their work (e.g., in public policy and law) or as voters and consumers.

- **Because of existing and new requirements for teacher certification in many states, lower-division undergraduate science and mathematics education will need to prepare the next generation of teachers more rigorously. The same faculty who teach these courses for pre-service students also will need to become more engaged with professional development for many practicing teachers.**
  If current projections hold, up to two million college graduates will be needed in the next decade to serve as grade K-12

"Not long ago, a college chemistry professor grew angry with the way her daughter's high school chemistry class was being taught. She made an appointment to meet with the teacher and marched with righteous indignation into the classroom—only to discover that the teacher was one of her own former students."

Yates, 1995, pg. 8B

---

teachers (Darling-Hammond, 1997). The quality of science and mathematics education that these graduates received as undergraduates could have a direct impact on the amount of mathematics or science their K-12 students study and may contribute to the level of student achievement in these subjects (e.g., mathematics: Hawkins et al., 1998; science: O'Sullivan et al., 1998; see also Education Trust, 1998). Many of these students will eventually enroll in the nation's colleges and universities. As called for in National Research Council and other reports, if inquiry-based and standards-based teaching and learning are increasingly accepted as the prevailing educational paradigms for K-12 education, postsecondary institutions will need to respond, especially by

including these techniques in the preparation of prospective teachers and the continuing education of current teachers.

The National Council of Teachers of Mathematics (1989, 1991), the American Association for the Advancement of Science (1993), and the National Research Council (1996b) all have contributed to high-quality national standards in K-12 science and mathematics. The International Technology Education Association has developed *Standards for Technology Education* (the publication of which is expected in early spring of 1999) in a complementary style to the previous standards efforts. To date, statewide curriculum frameworks have been enacted by more than 25 states (Council of Chief State School Officers, 1997). Like the national efforts, these state frameworks also define what students should know and be able to do in science, mathematics, and technology throughout the K-12 years.[4] These K-12 standards can assist undergraduate institutions in defining minimum entrance requirements in SME&T. These standards also could be used to restructure current standardized testing programs in mathematics and to construct standardized tests in science and technology that could be administered to *all* students who seek to pursue higher education. Thus, agencies such as the Educational Testing Service and the American College Testing Program could be important partners in and contributors to the improvement of undergraduate SME&T education.

- **Lower-division undergraduate science and mathematics education sets the stage for career scientists, mathematicians, and**

---

[4]Although no similar standards are being proposed for undergraduate education on a national scale, in the fall of 1997, the Education Trust in Washington, DC initiated a two-year project with public universities and community colleges from seven states to explore the possibility of establishing curricular standards in history and one of the natural sciences on each campus. The results of that initiative were not available at the time of publication of this report.

engineers who will become the next generation of postsecondary faculty. Of the students who pursue careers in science, mathematics, or engineering, a significant fraction become faculty members at the nation's two- and four-year colleges and universities. If current trends continue, many of these students will not have received even minimal training in the practice of teaching during their graduate or postdoctoral years. Instead, they will assume faculty positions with only vague knowledge about effective teaching practice, about the ways students learn, or about the literature that can inform them and help them improve their teaching.

Many of these new faculty members will use teaching practices that they themselves encountered as undergraduates. Future teachers who, in turn, take courses from these faculty also may adopt similar techniques to teach their own students, so a kind of cycle continues. Lack of background and skills in teaching, meager or nonexistent institutional programs for ongoing faculty development, and an academic culture that sometimes emphasizes performance in research more than in teaching are all factors that work against innovation in and new approaches to undergraduate SME&T instruction. Thus, the structure of graduate and postdoctoral programs directly influences the quality of undergraduate instruction in science and mathematics and, in turn, the future of K-12 SME&T education.

Breaking this cycle—or improving its outcome—is particularly important given recent studies that suggest that many students who enter colleges intent on becoming SME&T majors change their plans after taking introductory SME&T courses. Many of these students report that a major consideration in their decision to switch to other majors is the quality of teaching they encountered in those introductory courses (Seymour and Hewitt, 1997).

Thus, all SME&T faculty, departments, programs, and SME&T colleges should consider the following kinds of questions as they examine their SME&T education programs: Are we providing all of our students with the kinds of effective teaching techniques and meaningful educational experiences that truly excite them about SME&T? Do we actively engage students in SME&T in ways similar to how we work as scientists, mathematicians, or engineers, given that the vast majority of students in our introductory courses will never again have formal exposure to our disciplines? Are we providing them with the intellectual skills and background they will need to appreciate and continue learning about SME&T throughout their lives? Are we helping our students understand "real world" applications of SME&T? Do we make explicit connections between our disciplines and others in the natural sciences, social sciences, and the humanities in our courses and when advising students?

This Report

The conclusions and recommendations in this report of the National Research Council's Committee on Undergraduate Science and Education (CUSE) are based on five years of surveying the scholarly research on improving science education and discussions with faculty, administrators, higher education organizations, and other leaders in the higher education community, many of whom participated in the "Year of Dialogue" (see Appendix A). The emphasis of the report is on change in undergraduate SME&T education principally at the lower-division level for *all* students, not just those who will pursue a major in one of the SME&T disciplines. The need for change and how to accomplish it is articulated through a series of visions and strategies. Supporting evidence or background is given for each vision as well as for the strategies for implementing the required changes.

These strategies are directed to two primary audiences: 1) executive and academic officers and 2) individual faculty members and their departments. It is critical that academic administrators and faculty work collaboratively to address the issues articulated in this report. To help facilitate this process, these strategies are juxtaposed in the Executive Summary and elaborated in the main report.

The committee would like to emphasize, however, that in the dialogue that members hope will take place on college and university campuses after the release of this report, the voices of many people on campus will be heard. These voices should include not only those of chief academic officers and faculty in schools of education and in the SME&T disciplines but also directors of campus teaching and learning centers, information technology policy-makers, officers in SME&T disciplinary societies and education organizations, and graduate school faculty and deans.

CUSE members acknowledge that numerous local, regional, and national reform efforts to improve undergraduate SME&T education have been undertaken to date, and some high-quality programs are already in place. However, CUSE members contend that broader efforts are needed by all postsecondary institutions. Undergraduate SME&T education at all postsecondary institutions needs to be made accessible and relevant to more students. Teaching methods that recognize and accommodate the different learning styles of today's diverse student body need to be embraced. Postsecondary SME&T faculty should add value to *all* students' education by structuring courses in ways that allow students to gain deeper insights and understanding of the SME&T disciplines during their undergraduate experiences than they achieved in their pre-college years.

At present, many college-bound students have up to 12 years of exposure to various aspects of science and mathematics before entering college, but most do not take more than one year of courses in these subjects as undergraduates. This is despite the fact that many of them will then go on to pursue careers or other activities that require some

understanding and appreciation of the nature and limits of SME&T. No college or university can hope to make all of its students truly "literate" in the *content* of even one SME&T subdiscipline, given the rapid advances in virtually all areas of SME&T. However, postsecondary institutions can provide much better educational value for every undergraduate student by incorporating into the curriculum the concepts and methods of basic science, mathematical reasoning, technological application, the connections among these disciplines, and their relationship to societal concerns. Multidisciplinary or interdisciplinary courses and curricula can provide students with this increasingly important perspective of SME&T.

Readers will note that while this report, its visions, and many of its strategies address the breadth of undergraduate SME&T education, many of the report's examples of innovative practice are drawn from undergraduate science education. The committee would like to note here that many of the issues being debated in science education also apply to mathematics, engineering, and technology education. For example, the issues and recommendations addressed in *Engineering Education: Designing an Adaptive System* (National Research Council, 1995a) are quite congruent with the issues raised and the strategies for implementation in this report. In addition, many of the federal agencies that support science education (e.g., the National Science Foundation) are calling for greater integration among the disciplines. This report addresses the larger SME&T community in that spirit, as well.

Reaching students who will become teachers of grades K-12 and those who are unlikely to have further formal exposure to science or technology beyond their college years is especially important. Thus, every introductory SME&T course, regardless of student audience or type of postsecondary institution at which the course is offered, should stress the nature and applications of SME&T and the connections among these disciplines in addition to the content associated with a particular discipline. Here again, a multidisciplinary approach to teaching and learning about SME&T could be valuable, especially for this population of students.

After reading this report, one might reasonably ask whether undergraduate education in SME&T could possibly be transformed to the extent proposed by the committee. The committee believes that it can be, largely because of the inherent academic strength of our colleges and universities and the nationwide interest in improving education: these both offer an unparalleled opportunity for all postsecondary institutions to provide the kind of quality SME&T education that all undergraduates need.

Individual colleges and universities need not address the issues involved in isolation. Innovative courses, curricula, and pedagogical approaches are already being developed and tested at many types of colleges and universities across the United States. Our highest elected and appointed leaders, public and private foundations, and prominent research scientists and policy-makers have identified SME&T literacy for all students at the pre-college and undergraduate levels as a top priority for the nation. Specific recommendations for action are available (e.g., Clinton and Gore, 1994; National Academy of Sciences, 1997; National Research Council, 1982, 1989, 1991, 1995a, 1996a; National Science Foundation, 1996b; Howard Hughes Medical Institute, 1995, 1996a), and many funding sources (both public and private) are now providing considerable financial support to catalyze innovation and change in undergraduate SME&T education (e.g., Howard Hughes Medical Institute, 1996b; National Science Foundation, 1998a).

A GOAL AND AN AGENDA

FOR TRANSFORMING UNDERGRADUATE EDUCATION IN SCIENCE, MATHEMATICS, ENGINEERING, AND TECHNOLOGY

Based on research and extensive dialogue with representatives of many sectors of the SME&T higher education community, the members of the Committee on Undergraduate Science Education (CUSE) call for the following to become a **primary goal** of individual institutional efforts to reform SME&T undergraduate education:

Institutions of higher education should provide diverse opportunities for *all* undergraduates to study science, mathematics, engineering, and technology as practiced by scientists and engineers, and as early in their academic careers as possible.

This statement explicitly includes students who do not plan to declare majors in the natural sciences, mathematics, or engineering and is meant to give special emphasis to those students who will become teachers of science and mathematics for grades K-12. It implies that changes necessary to the improvement of undergraduate SME&T education must begin with a reexamination and fundamental restructuring of introductory and lower level courses and programs at both two- and four-year postsecondary institutions. Achieving lasting reform at any level in education is an exceedingly complex task that must engage virtually all components and every type of institution within the system. Students who enroll in SME&T courses, individual faculty, academic depart ments (both within and outside of the natural

sciences and engineering), service units (academic support units and physical plants), and the academic, executive, and financial leaders within a given institution of higher educational will be affected.

Reaching the Goal: An Agenda

Contained in this report are six summary vision statements constructed by the members of CUSE. They are based on extensive consultation with representatives of the higher education community and an extensive survey of the research literature. These visions are in full accord with previously published reports and studies on undergraduate SME&T education. Overview and background sections for each vision statement provide further information about the basis of and rationale for each statement. CUSE members deemed it critical to provide specific strategies for implementing each of the six vision statements. These appear after the background sections and provide specific approaches and resources that can be used by chief academic officers, faculty members, and academic units individually and collectively to effect change on their own campuses.

CUSE's mandate was to find ways to improve undergraduate science education for all undergraduates. The committee responded by focusing most of its time and effort in understanding what individual faculty and departments could do to foster change, and this emphasis is reflected in the amount of text associated with **Vision 2**. However, as the committee pursued its work, it became apparent that undergraduate education also must be considered as an integral part of the continuum of education in the United States that extends from pre-kindergarten through the graduate and postdoctoral years. The order in which the vision statements and strategies for implementation are presented in this report reflects that continuum.

Innovative, effective undergraduate SME&T education depends, in part, on having students matriculate at postsecondary institutions who have had sufficient pre-college educational experiences to enable them to undertake college-level work. Therefore, **Vision 1** addresses pre-college preparation and the changes that are occurring in K-12 science and mathematics education.

Vision 2 then focuses on the roles and responsibilities of postsecondary faculty and SME&T curricula. Postsecondary faculty add value to students' pre-college educational experiences by making explicit to students the connections among the natural science disciplines and by providing opportunities for students to understand the processes and limits of science through inquiry-based and interdisciplinary approaches to teaching and learning. For science majors, this exposure might often involve participation in undergraduate research.

Next, **Vision 3** addresses the importance of designing courses and programs that can be appropriately evaluated for their effectiveness in advancing the learning of SME&T by lower-division undergraduate students.

Vision 4 goes on to address explicitly the needs of two critically important groups of students—undergraduates who enroll in SME&T courses (especially at the introductory level) and who may go on to become teachers of science and mathematics in grades K-12 and practicing teachers of science and mathematics in grades K-12. For too long, the education of future teachers as well as the continuing professional development of current science and mathematics teachers have been viewed by many faculty in SME&T disciplines as primarily the responsibilities of

schools of education. **Vision 4** calls on faculty in the natural sciences and engineering to become more directly involved in developing integrated approaches to the preparation and continuing professional development of K-12 teachers.

Vision 5 considers the role of institutions in catalyzing change in undergraduate SME&T education through the provision of appropriate rewards and incentives to faculty, creation and support of other institutional resources, such as Teaching and Learning Centers, and assistance to faculty in engaging in appropriate planning for facilities and equipment.

Finally, **Vision 6** examines the future of undergraduate SME&T education by considering the role of graduate and postdoctoral education in preparing the next generation of college and university faculty to become skilled teachers. It also addresses the need to support current faculty in learning more about how teaching methods affect student learning.

Many of the specific strategies for implementation in this report expand and build upon the issues articulated in a convocation and subsequent report entitled *From Analysis to Action: Undergraduate Education in Science, Mathematics, Engineering, and Technology* (National Research Council, 1996a) and in national hearings and the subsequent report entitled *Shaping the Future: New Expectations for Undergraduate Education in Science, Mathematics, Engineering, and Technology* (National Science Foundation, 1996b). They reflect the "Year of Dialogue" held across the country by this report's authoring committee with a broad range of postsecondary representatives. Taken together, these implementation strategies could lead to fundamental, systemic improvement in the many facets of undergraduate SME&T education.

The vision statements and their attendant implementation strategies have been provided primarily for those who work directly with undergraduates across the broad spectrum of postsecondary institutions in the United States. Thus, the principles are relevant to community colleges, liberal arts colleges, comprehensive universities, and research universities. When the roles of graduate and post-doctoral programs are addressed, as in **Vision 6**, it is as they pertain to undergraduate education.

The committee recognizes that not all of the recommendations and strategies for implementation will be equally useful or applicable to all postsecondary institutions. Different institutional histories, patterns of governance, campus cultures, and efforts to date to improve undergraduate education may make some implementation strategies more useful than others for a given institution. For example, many of the strategies for implementing **Vision 6** (changes in graduate and postdoctoral programs) will not apply to community colleges and four-year undergraduate institutions. However, the committee believes that most SME&T departments and institutions should be able to utilize or adopt many of the implementation strategies offered in the report. The committee also recommends that all SME&T programs at two- and four-year colleges and universities work with other professional schools on campus that have direct or indirect interests in SME&T education (e.g., education, medical, business, and law schools), with programs in

the humanities and social sciences, and with SME&T departments at other institutions in their regions.

Since large numbers of undergraduates now begin their higher education careers at community colleges and then matriculate at four-year institutions or move directly to the workplace (National Science Foundation, 1997a), two- and four-year institutions, educational associations, and local businesses and industries must work closely together at the local, state, and national levels to develop comprehensive plans for improving undergraduate SME&T education.

Changing the status quo is always difficult. When such change challenges the current organizational structure and mission of postsecondary institutions, strong leadership, understanding, and support for change will have to come from the top officials of those institutions to encourage the faculty who are working to improve SME&T education. Adopting the visions and implementing the strategies for change that are provided in this report will require a great deal of commitment, time, and creative energy by faculty, departments, and academic administrative leaders.

VISIONS

FOR UNDERGRADUATE EDUCATION IN SCIENCE, MATHEMATICS, ENGINEERING, AND TECHNOLOGY

VISION 1

All postsecondary institutions would require all entering students to undertake college-level studies in SME&T. Entry into higher education would include assessment of students' understanding of these subjects that is based on the recommendations of national K-12 standards.

If undergraduates are to view SME&T as an integral component of their education, the stage should be set long before they enter college. Ideally, their pre-college experience should have included both quality instruction in standards-based classrooms and a clear awareness that achievement in science, mathematics, and technology will be expected for admission to college. Once implemented, standards-based approaches to science and mathematics (and eventually technology) education should enable more students to reach these desired levels of achievement.

However, the committee recognizes that standards-based K-12 education in science, mathematics, and technology is not yet available to most students across the country. Many colleges and universities must now rely on the results of standardized examinations in these disciplines that do not necessarily emphasize the kinds of learning called for in national standards. Many postsecondary institutions also employ open admission policies. Such policies provide critical educational opportunities to many students who may not have had the academic experiences called for by national and state standards.

Moving K-12 SME&T education to a system that is more consonant with standards will likely require at least a decade. Nevertheless, change is occurring—albeit at different rates— in many parts of the country, and increasing numbers of students are likely to arrive at postsecondary institutions with greater exposure to science and mathematics standards. Thus, postsecondary institutions, their admissions offices, and faculty will need to monitor these trends in K-12 education with respect to admissions policies and the content and teaching of undergraduate courses. Admissions policies should be revisited regularly to account for changes taking place in the K-12 sector.

The committee also recognizes that while this vision and the accompanying implementation strategies are appropriate for the great majority of students in the nation's high schools, many other students will need creative alternative pathways to higher education. These students include those who have not performed well academically in high school but who have potential to succeed at college-level studies and those who did not receive the kind of education articulated in this report and who, as adults, are now seeking additional education.

Background

K-12 science and mathematics standards are being implemented across the country (National Council of Teachers of Mathematics, 1989; American Association for the Advancement of Science, 1993; National Research Council, 1996b). Curriculum frameworks and learning results in science and mathematics are now legislatively mandated by many states based on these national standards and benchmarks (Council of Chief State School Officers, 1997). These standards call for students increasingly to engage in inquiry-based, collaborative learning experiences that emphasize observation, collection, and analysis of data from student-oriented experiments. They also stress the importance of helping students learn about the relationships among the sciences and the relevance of science, mathematics, and technology to other realms of inquiry and practice.

At present, not all K-12 students receive an acceptable preparation in science and mathematics at the pre-college level. For example, in the most recent National Assessment of Educational Progress examinations in mathematics, about one in three students in grades 4 and 8 and slightly less than one in three (31%) in grade 12 could not demonstrate even the most basic competency, and only 5% or less performed at the advanced level (e.g., Reese et al., 1997). In the most recent relevant international study, students from the United States demonstrated a steady decline from the 4th through the 12th grade in their mathematics and science performance. By 12th grade, American students ranked near the bottom in every category for knowledge of both general and advanced levels of science and mathematics in the Third International Mathematics and Science Study (TIMSS) compared with their counterparts in countries around the world (U.S. Department of Education, 1998a, although see Rotberg, 1998[5]).

Students who do arrive at college with what traditionally has been considered good preparation in science and mathematics (e.g., Advanced Placement course work) may not have actually developed a real conceptual understanding or the ability to solve problems, particularly in mathematics and the physical sciences, when compared with students in other countries with similar educational backgrounds (Juillerat et al., 1997; U.S. Department of Education, 1998a). Yet, at present, in the United States, students with Advanced Placement (AP) credits and high AP exam scores in hand can sometimes avoid any further science or mathematics classes at the postsecondary level that would lead them to think about SME&T subject matter more deeply.[6]

The clear national need for SME&T competency has helped drive the development and implementation of standards for K-12 mathematics and science (with technology standards anticipated in the spring of 1999). These standards present institutions of higher education with a great opportunity

- to better define what they expect students to know and be able to do in SME&T as a requirement of admission; and to

- institute their own innovative approaches to the teaching and learning of science, mathematics, and technology that complement and extend those called for in the standards.

The implications of changes in admissions policies include

- assisting students and their parents to understand the value of SME&T competency for all students pursuing any career direction; and

---

[5]The Third International Mathematics and Science Study (TIMSS) represents the most extensive investigation of mathematics and science education ever conducted. Approximately 50 countries participated in this comparative survey of education focusing on nine- and thirteen-year-old students and students in their last year of secondary school. For the oldest students, TIMSS analyses considered three groups: a cross section of all students completing their last year of secondary education, i.e., a "literacy" sample; mathematics specialists, i.e., those students studying or having studied calculus; and science specialists, i.e., those students studying or having studied physics. (Modified from information available from the U.S. National Research

Center for TIMSS. More information about this examination is available at <http://ustimss.msu.edu/>. There have been differences of opinion about the TIMSS assessments, particularly at the 12th grade level, where the results have been challenged based on perceived deficiencies in the collection and statistical analyses of the data (Rotberg, 1998). In a response to Rotberg, the methods employed in the TIMSS study have been defended by Schmidt and McKnight (1998).

[6]Advanced Placement (AP) credits and high AP examination scores can allow some students to complete or waive specific college graduation requirements, including in science and mathematics, at some postsecondary institutions.

- opportunities for faculty in the SME&T disciplines to work more closely with their admissions officers, college administrators, pre-college standardized testing agencies, and accrediting bodies to better define specific competencies.[7]

Strategies for Promoting and Implementing Vision 1

Executive and academic officers of postsecondary institutions can implement Vision 1 by

1. Asking academic SME&T departments and the Office of Admissions to establish appropriate institutional admissions standards for science and mathematics preparation.

The NCTM *Curriculum and Evaluation Standards for School Mathematics*, AAAS *Benchmarks for Science Literacy*, the NRC *National Science Education Standards*, and individual state curriculum frameworks and learning results have established a "floor" for the level of knowledge and competency that should be mastered by students in science and mathematics before and during the high-school years. Concomitantly, institutions of higher education should set higher standards for their entering students. These standards should be consistent with the program goals of the institution and institutional missions, as well as with state standards or benchmarks. A requirement or admissions preference for four years each of science and mathematics in high school may be appropriate for many postsecondary institutions and would send a powerful message to students, parents, and schools about the importance of these subjects. If colleges, universities, university systems, or organizations representing groups of universities decide to expect this type of higher level of background and competency from entering students, this expectation should be

communicated early and clearly to high schools and to the public at-large.

Individual faculty and academic departments can implement Vision 1 by

1. Responding to both the current educational experiences and accomplishments of today's students and the changing expectations about what pre-college students should know and should be able to do in SME&T as a result of the increased use of national and statewide standards-based curricula and assessment tools.

As national and statewide standards in science and mathematics are articulated and implemented, students who enter the nation's colleges and universities will have very different knowledge bases and skills. Their expectations for continued study in SME&T subjects will be very different as well. For example, students are likely to expect class sizes that are much smaller than those of many undergraduate lecture sections. In addition, they might expect laboratory exercises to be integrated with the topics being learned in the lecture section. Large lecture sections for introductory courses that at best offer non-integrated lab experiences will not be familiar to these students. That the majority of the states have already adopted standards-based curricula and assessment tools should be taken as an early warning sign to individual faculty and departments that they need to prepare for the changes that standards will bring. Faculty and departments could prepare by reading and discussing the implications of national and relevant state standards for the structuring of courses, programs, and assessment of student learning and progress at the postsecondary level. The discussions could include experts in science and mathematics education research and practice, such as faculty from schools of education

2. Working with their institution's Office of Admissions to make clear to prospective students the departments' expectations for entry into SME&T programs and the institution's goal

---

[7]A number of state university systems already are working with the K-12 communities in their states to make their admission policies more consistent with alternative methods for assessing pre-college student performance (e.g., University of Wisconsin System, 1997; Oregon University System, 1998).

of providing SME&T education to all of its enrolled students.

The Office of Admissions should be equipped to send clear signals to prospective students about the kinds of preparation they should have in order to succeed in college-level SME&T courses and programs (e.g., President and Fellows of Harvard University, 1993).

Every effort should be made to encourage students to undertake a rigorous high-school program of studies, including Advanced Placement (AP) courses where they are available. However, in working with the Office of Admissions, departments also should decide whether AP examinations actually measure the breadth and depth of knowledge and understanding about both the subject matter in question and the processes of science in general that students would otherwise acquire from taking introductory SME&T courses at the university level. For example, not all AP courses in the sciences offer the same level of laboratory experience for students. Students with the same scores on AP examinations may have had vastly different levels of exposure to scientific instrumentation or to approaches for solving problems in a laboratory setting.

If the mission of postsecondary education is to provide students with opportunities to experience and think about subject matter more deeply than they could in high school, allowing some students to *complete or waive* specific graduation requirements on the basis of high AP examination scores alone (compared, for example, with awarding them credit toward the total number of credits required for graduation) could be self-defeating to that mission.[8] Requiring **all** students

to complete introductory, interdisciplinary, or higher level courses in SME&T, regardless of their intended major, would enable some of the best students in the university to experience and appreciate the wealth and breadth of the sciences that they otherwise might have missed during their high school years. In collaboration with the Office of Admissions, departments should make clear how SME&T departments will regard students with high scores on these examinations, especially those who wish to use these scores to avoid taking college-level mathematics or science courses (also, see footnote 6, page 22). Detailed information about the kinds of experiences a student's AP course provided should be considered along with that student's score on an AP examination for placement in advanced courses or the awarding of academic credit.

In the near future, students who have had a standards-based education at the pre-college level, where they engaged in inquiry-based, collaborative learning experiences, will expect to receive more of the same in their undergraduate science and mathematics courses. Postsecondary institutions that take the lead in offering undergraduate SME&T curricula of high value to all of their students not only will have highly successful graduates but also will attract the highest quality incoming students.

The national need for SME&T competency is a great opportunity for institutions of higher education to institute meaningful, substantive change in the ways these subjects are taught. In addition, standards-based approaches to education also could allow postsecondary institutions to better define what they expect students to know and be able to do in SME&T as requirements for admission to higher education. However, if meaningful change is to occur in admissions policies, faculty in the SME&T disciplines at two- and four-year institutions will have to work more closely with each other and with their institutions' admissions officers and administrators as

[8]Even high scores on these examinations cannot necessarily be equated with this desired level of understanding. The recent Third International Mathematics and Science Study (TIMSS) results for 12th graders suggest that, at least for mathematics and the physical sciences, many students in the United States who are doing Advanced Placement work in these subjects do not demonstrate real conceptual understanding or ability to solve problems within these disciplines compared to students in other countries with similar educational backgrounds (U.S. Department of Education, 1998a, although see Rotberg, 1998).

well as with pre-college standardized testing agencies and accrediting bodies to better define specific competencies.

*See Appendix A for additional information about strategies for implementation of **Vision 1** as discussed during the Committee on Undergraduate Science Education's "Year of Dialogue" regional symposia and topical forums.*

VISION 2

SME&T would become an integral part of the curriculum for all undergraduate students through required introductory courses that engage all students in SME&T and their connections to society and the human condition.

Science is an integral part of our daily lives. It also is an historical and procedural foundation for human thinking about and understanding of the natural and engineered worlds. Therefore, colleges and universities should require *all* entering students, irrespective of their ultimate selection of a major, to undertake college-level studies in SME&T. Science majors would gain a focused, in-depth exposure to scientific principles, and those who wished to do so could build on their experiences to participate in faculty-supervised original research. They and all non-science students would also enroll in courses that focus on providing awareness, understanding, and appreciation of the natural and human-constructed worlds and that involve at least one laboratory experience. Introductory undergraduate curricula would incorporate physical, biological, and mathematical sciences, engineering, and technology in a manner that allowed all students to understand and appreciate the interrelationships among these disciplines in the context of human society. All of these courses would include topics that are both intellectually challenging and near the frontiers of inquiry.

Wherever possible, these topics would engage students in discussing problems that students would find timely and important.

If this vision were to be realized, faculty would design and offer introductory science courses that met the needs of students with diverse educational backgrounds, experiences, interests, aspirations, and learning styles. These courses would be high-quality, laboratory-rich experiences that are meaningful and appropriate for all undergraduate students regardless of their intended majors. In addition to presenting content information in one or more areas of science, these courses would engage undergraduates in exploring the fundamental and unifying concepts and processes of science. They would be interdisciplinary in nature and focus, providing case studies that examine real problems and applications. They would emphasize the evolving processes of scientific thought and inquiry and would encourage and assist students to understand the need to be lifelong learners of SME&T. In short, these lower-division courses would be designed in content and subject matter approach in such a way as to encourage many students to continue to advance, rather than to end, their SME&T study; that is, the courses would serve as "pumps" to, rather than "filters" out of, higher levels of study in SME&T.

The creation and support of innovative courses also would include the building of a sophisticated communications infrastructure so that students, faculty, and local, state, national, and international communities could share ideas, strategies, and solutions for richer, more genuine educational experiences. Collectively, this communications network (constructed primarily on the Internet) would deepen the reform of undergraduate SME&T courses. An important contribution would be the effective use of information technologies in SME&T curricula.[9]

---

[9]The NRC's Committee on Information Technology, under the auspices of the Center for Science, Mathematics, and Engineering Education, anticipates concluding by the spring of 1999 a study on effective, appropriate use of information technology to enhance SME&T courses. More information on this project can be found at the National Academy of Sciences' home page, <http://www.nas.edu>, under "Current Projects."

In addition, *all* programs in SME&T would be structured to allow as many undergraduate students as possible to engage in original, supervised research under the tutelage of a faculty or senior graduate student mentor. Undergraduates would become involved with as many phases of a research project as time permitted. These might include experimental design, searching the literature, performing the research using modern scientific instruments and techniques, analyzing and interpreting data, and preparing a report for publication or presentation at an institutional, regional, or national scientific meeting. SME&T majors would undertake such research for a minimum of one academic term, although research experiences that last for longer periods of time would be encouraged whenever possible. Other students, especially those who aspire to careers in teaching, would be encouraged to participate in original research, either through inquiry-based laboratory experiences associated with SME&T courses or through the kinds of supervised research opportunities available to SME&T majors. For research experiences lasting one semester or less, students might become involved with faculty- or student-originated projects in progress or with smaller projects designed by a faculty member and a group of students in a research-based course.

Background

Traditionally, the education of science majors has been hierarchical for several reasons. First, it has been thought that students in science must acquire a solid background in mathematics before approaching traditional introductory courses in physics and chemistry. Second, because many scientific disciplines have relied on other sciences as cognates (e.g., chemistry programs require their students also to study physics), the first order of business has been for students to gain prerequisite, college-level knowledge of these subjects, forcing delay in or eliminating consideration of topics related to the

applications and appreciation of science in a broader context. Third, it has been assumed that students who major in a science will take a sequence of courses that can be spread over several years.

This vertical structuring of course content sometimes has had the effect of reducing introductory and intermediate courses to what students perceive to be litanies of facts. Conceptual knowledge, broader understanding of challenging subject matter, and more comprehensive approaches to teaching and learning, such as consideration of applications and intellectual and societal issues, too often has been minimized or postponed until the end of the course (e.g., Tobias, 1992). Also neglected at these levels of instruction have been the interrelationships among the sciences and the sciences' relationship to the humanities, social sciences, and the political, economic, and social concerns of society. Applications of scientific principles and integration of these concepts with those from other disciplines too often has been delayed until the junior or senior year (and sometimes not considered at all) because many faculty have believed that students should obtain a strong grounding in the basic principles first (Tobias, 1992).

In short, the traditional first-year exposure to a single discipline course has given students, especially those who do not go on in SME&T, an incomplete view of how the discipline applies to them, their physical or social environments, and their futures. As for declared and prospective science majors, although many take courses in more than one discipline at a time (taking biology and chemistry simultaneously, for example), explicit connections between even these disciplines are not always made. If such connections are made in the course of the undergraduate experience as presently constructed, it is later, in upper-division levels.

While sequencing of information and concepts makes sense, the committee suggests that the sequence should take place in an alternative fashion. Students should obtain a strong but broad grounding in SME&T first. Then, if they so choose, students can become better versed in more specific and narrow concepts as they advance through their undergraduate careers. Although there have been numerous attempts to restructure undergraduate science education *within disciplines* (e.g., in the chemical sciences: American Chemical Society, 1990; in the earth sciences: Ireton et al., 1996; in engineering: National Research Council, 1995a; in the life sciences: Coalition for Education in the Life Sciences, 1992, and Biological Sciences Curriculum Study, 1993; in the mathematical sciences: National Research Council, 1991; in the physical sciences: Arons, 1990, Wilson, 1996, and Redish and Rigden, 1997), there have been few systemic efforts to restructure introductory courses for science majors, pre-service teachers, and students who will go on to other academic pursuits.

There are many reasons to reconstitute the courses under discussion so that they emphasize applications and connections with other areas of knowledge (National Research Council, 1982, 1996a; Cheney, 1989; American Association for the Advancement of Science, 1990; Tobias, 1990; Hazen and Trefil, 1991; National Science Foundation, 1992, 1996b; Alberts, 1994; Jones, 1994; Project Kaleidoscope, 1991, 1997; Boyer Commission on Educating Undergraduates in the Research University, 1998). First, the proposed interdisciplinary courses provide integrated perspectives of SME&T and its relationship to the human condition in a way that invites student involvement and active participation. Second, such courses also serve as gateways to more discipline-based subjects by allowing students to understand the importance of studying what might otherwise seem to be disconnected and unrelated topics. When such interdisciplinary courses are reserved for upper-level science majors, non-science majors (including future teachers) cannot benefit from them. It is the latter group for

"My own experience leads me to conclude that it is pointless to define scientific literacy in terms of any particular body of scientific knowledge. I neither know nor understand most of present-day science. And yet, I am a dean of science at a private college, an active researcher, and the author of several mathematics textbooks and science books for the general reader. I read journals, magazines, and books about science. Indeed, my life revolves around it. But scientific knowledge has been advancing at such a pace since the Second World War that I cannot hope to keep up. No one can . . . It is neither possible nor necessary for the general population to have detailed scientific knowledge across a range of disciplines. Instead, what is important is *scientific awareness* . . . When I say that all adults should be scientifically aware, I mean that they should base their opinions on fact and observable evidence rather than on prejudice or assumptions; be willing to change their opinions based on new evidence; understand cause-and-effect relationships; and appreciate how science is done (in particular, understand the role played by observation and experiment in establishing a scientific conclusion and know what the terms "scientific theory" and "scientific fact" mean. My long experience as a college educator has shown me that, despite the near ubiquity of science-and-mathematics requirements for a bachelor's degree, not even all college graduates meet these standards for scientific awareness. (Nor do most college professors, for that matter.)"

Devlin, 1998, pg. B6

which such approaches to teaching SME&T may be especially appropriate.

The committee appreciates that a considerable amount of time must be devoted to preparing for and teaching such courses. Time spent in courses discussing integrated topics will limit the amount of other subject matter that can be covered. However, the value of an integrated approach for most students over the long term is likely to outweigh these challenges. Furthermore, if students'

"Why are the head of the Environmental Protection Agency, the Ambassador to Kazakhastan (a country with concerns over earthquakes, oil reserves, and nuclear contamination), and the chairman of the House Science Committee not scientists? Why are we not training scientists for the leadership positions that so profoundly affect our future? It starts with universities, where success has historically been achieved through specialization in narrow subdisciplines. Courses for nonmajors are frequently viewed as distractions, and students who depart the so-called nerd herd to pursue careers in business or policy-making are frowned upon. Thus begins the vicious cycle: Bright students do not see science as a way to reach positions of leadership, and science suffers because those in leadership positions have little experience with science . . . Our long-term future depends on citizens understanding and appreciating the role of science in our society. No panel report, no unambiguous example, and no well-connected lobbyist can make these arguments for us. In the next generation, we will need not only scientists who are experts in subspecialties, but also those with a broad understanding of science and a basic literacy in economics, international affairs, and policy-making. In the end, our greatest threat may not be the scientific illiteracy of the public, but the political illiteracy of scientists."

van der Vink, 1997

interest in SME&T is piqued by this approach, they may want to enroll in additional upper-level, discipline-based courses.

The committee again emphasizes that it is impossible for any student to become truly "literate" in SME&T if "literacy" is equated with "content" in one or more disciplines. Postsecondary SME&T programs can, however, provide all students who enroll in these courses with firm foundations in the concepts and methods of basic science and technology, mathematical reasoning, the

connections among these fields and methods of inquiry, and the relationship of these fields to other disciplines and to addressing societal concerns.

Upper-division interdisciplinary courses for science majors typically are taught by faculty colleagues within closely related disciplines to students who have majored in those same disciplines. In contrast, at the introductory level, faculty from different departments may not have the same level of motivation to work together coordinating and integrating SME&T courses (Tobias, 1992; Boyer Commission on Educating Undergraduates in the Research University, 1998). At present, there are few truly interdisciplinary courses offered at the introductory level. Reasons for this include lack of course ownership by any one department or discipline or a dearth of commitment by faculty or administrators to the course or program. Students who have not enrolled previously in such courses might be reluctant to take what they perceive to be a non-traditional approach to the subject matter at hand, and departments may interpret this reluctance as lack of interest. Faculty rarely can see a direct relationship of such courses to their individual research interests and may receive few incentives from the institution's system of rewards and recognition for devoting the time, retraining, and effort required to develop high-quality interdisciplinary courses. This problem is exacerbated when the courses are intended primarily for students who will not pursue advanced study in the faculty's own department or programs. If individual faculty or departments see little reason to expend the effort and resources to make innovative, relevant courses available, students who are not science majors can hardly be expected to be enthusiastic about the more traditional courses that are available to them. Non-science majors who exhibit a lack of interest in courses designed primarily for science majors may reinforce faculty or departmental resistance to making the effort to change and to offer more innovative introductory courses.

Interest in offering interdisciplinary courses at both the introductory and more advanced undergraduate levels has risen in recent years. Many workshops have been sponsored by Project Kaleidoscope to explore such diverse topics as "Blueprints for Reform in Undergraduate Neuroscience," "Connecting Within and Beyond the Sciences," and "Biochemistry: Bio or Chemistry?" (more information about these and other workshops is available at Project Kaleidoscope's website at <http://www.pkal.org>). In addition, "Interdisciplinary Learning Communities on Puget Sound" is organized to develop faculty skills in leading interdisciplinary programs. It will culminate in 1999 with a public symposium to present and discuss participants' work on curriculum and collaborative research. (More information is available at The Evergreen State College's Washington Center for Improving the Quality of Undergraduate Education website at <http://192.211.16.13/ katlinks/wash cntr/home.html>.)

The following are examples of interdisciplinary courses for students, although it should be noted that few course offerings of this type have been evaluated fully for efficacy: "Science and Society," offered at the University of California, Davis (<http://www. ucdavis.edu>); "Connecting the Sciences," offered at Nassau Community College (<http://www.sunynassau.edu/>); "The Explanatory Power of Science," offered at the University of Texas at El Paso (<http://www. utep.edu>); "Quantitative Perspectives on Energy and the Environment," offered at the University of Pennsylvania (<http://www. upenn.edu>); and "The Science and Technology of Everyday Life," offered at Hope College (<http://www.hope.edu>). One course-based textbook is *Science Matters: Achieving Scientific Literacy* (Hazen and Trefil, 1991), which encourages interdisciplinary study at the undergraduate level for non-majors by building connections between disciplines.

"As research is increasingly interdisciplinary, undergraduate education should also be cast in interdisciplinary formats. Departmental confines and reward structures have discouraged young faculty interested in interdisciplinary teaching from engaging in it. But because all work will require mental flexibility, students need to view their studies through many lenses. Many students come to the university with some introduction to interdisciplinary learning from high school and from use of computers. Once in college, they should find it possible to create individual majors or minors without undue difficulty. Understanding the close relationship between research and classroom learning, universities must seriously focus on ways to create interdisciplinarity in undergraduate learning."

Boyer Commission on Educating Undergraduates in the Research University, 1998, pg. 23

"Every citizen ought to be technologically literate. This includes not only scientific and mathematical literacy but also understanding the economic, social, and political roles that technology plays in society and the process by which technology is created . . . To be technologically literate, schoolchildren need to understand both the process and the products of engineering. They should be able to use basic mathematics and science skills to design solutions to problems. They also should be familiar with the methods that engineers use to evaluate design alternatives in search of the one that best satisfies constraints related to cost, functionality, safety, reliability, manufacturability, ergonomics, and environmental impact . . . People rely on technology for transportation, communication, medical care, entertainment, the food they eat, the clothing they wear, the buildings they use, and the work they do. Ignorance about such a fundamental feature of modern life is not healthy for individuals or for societies."

Wulf, 1998

Strategies for Promoting and Implementing Vision 2

Executive and academic officers of postsecondary institutions can implement Vision 2 by

1. At institutions with active research programs, convening local blue-ribbon panels of faculty who are recognized for their contributions to both research and teaching to report on what is needed to offer a cutting-edge SME&T curriculum for undergraduates on their campuses consistent with their institutions' mission.

The panel's report should provide a series of concrete short-term and long-term goals for the institution to pursue. Such discussions might include learning outcomes expected from introductory SME&T courses regardless of the course in which a student enrolls; greater opportunities for students to undertake original or independent research in teaching laboratories or in conjunction with faculty research projects; ways to enhance teacher preparation in mathematics, science, and technology; and the influence of K-12 standards-based curricula on undergraduate education in SME&T. Broader campus discussion about implementation, led by members of the panel and one or more high-ranking academic administrative officers, should follow release of the report.

2. Supporting the inclusion of core SME&T requirements and core course offerings that include at least one or preferably more laboratory experiences at the undergraduate level for all students and an option for independent research for all science majors.

All colleges and universities should critically evaluate their core SME&T requirements for undergraduate degrees and their core course offerings in these subjects. Departments other than those offering these courses should participate. The subjects of the evaluation should be the course content of each course and the development, integration, and financing of the total curriculum.

Faculty (and departments) should be given financial and other incentives to offer integrated, interdisciplinary courses at the introductory level and/or to coordinate the content and sequence of science courses with other introductory courses that beginning students are likely to take. For example, many first-year premedical students are likely to enroll simultaneously in introductory biology and chemistry. Instructors could present shared themes in these courses (e.g., properties and use of energy in chemical and biological systems) in a coordinated fashion and could refer to more specific material being covered in the other course. Beginning students would then have an early opportunity to see important connections usually not made until later in their undergraduate years. Graduate students, postdoctoral fellows, and selected undergraduates could participate in teaching (especially in laboratories) and in the development and assessment of such courses, thus helping faculty members make the most effective use of their resources. By seeking and using input from a diverse set of students (both undergraduates and graduates), faculty also would be able to modify more regularly the material presented and the methods of presentation. The adoption of new laboratory courses, which are critical for the teaching of science as an active way of learning, needs serious resource commitments from postsecondary institutions.

3. Encouraging individual faculty to learn to develop new and innovative courses and make existing courses more effective by promoting an institutional culture that rewards this participation and that provides technical support.

Most faculty members have been educated in traditional disciplines, and their teaching careers are usually traditional as well. To encourage these faculty to learn new and effective approaches to teaching and to develop new courses or curricula based on this knowledge, administrators should provide faculty with the resources required for consultation with colleagues and experts across campus and at other institutions. Faculty who then want to develop courses that are appropriate for all students should receive additional support.

Academic officers might make funds available directly to faculty who submit brief proposals to develop and teach high-quality, laboratory-rich interdisciplinary courses at the introductory level. Centralizing funds within the dean's office for such purposes also sends a powerful message about the need for faculty from different departments and disciplines to work together to procure these resources.

Deans and provosts also should tangibly recognize faculty members who develop and teach effective and innovative courses. Academic officers who oversee personnel decisions should adopt policies that show faculty that engaging students in truly innovative courses will be considered favorably in matters of tenure, promotion, and salary determinations. Such policies would encourage pre-tenured faculty to use innovative design and assessment of introductory courses as evidence of their productivity as teacher-scholars.

4. Providing incentives for individual faculty and departments in SME&T, the humanities, and the social sciences to work together to develop introductory interdisciplinary courses that are meaningful for *all* students, including both those who are and who are not likely to major in the faculty members' disciplines.

These courses might deal with broad issues, such as the environment, energy, or the impact of some aspect of SME&T on society. In addition to providing a solid grounding in some discrete body of scientific knowledge and content (to be determined by the course instructors), introductory courses also should impart deeper understanding of the processes and analytical tools of science and of the relationship of science to environmental, societal, or personal issues that students are likely to encounter (see examples beginning on page 33). To produce such courses, SME&T faculty from different disciplines should be encouraged to work together and

with colleagues in the humanities and social sciences to develop courses that provide students with broader exposure to and perspectives of the relationships among these areas of knowledge. Students should be encouraged (or even required) to enroll in one or more of these introductory interdisciplinary courses early in their undergraduate experience.

"... It is not enough that individual faculty members in isolated ways advance student learning. Many . . . have suggested that what we need is not *more innovation* but *more implementation*, so that local improvements are both spread throughout the institution and made sustainable over time. Otherwise, gains will be transitory and depend on the comings and goings of individual faculty and administrators."

National Science Foundation (1996b), pg. 56

---

5. Encouraging senior SME&T faculty who have been recognized for teaching excellence and innovation to participate in lower-division course offerings and in curriculum planning.

Too often the faculty members with the most experience and recognition as teacher-scholars instruct graduate students or advanced undergraduate students (Boyer Commission on Educating Undergraduates in the Research University, 1998). Thus, the vast majority of students who do not go on to upper-division courses or research in SME&T cannot benefit from interacting closely with and learning from the people who may be able to most inspire and guide their thinking in these disciplines. As the Boyer Commission points out, interactions between experienced teacher-scholars and bright, energetic students can catalyze and energize the thinking of both. Even if such teaching responsibilities do not become a requirement, senior faculty who are recognized for their teaching skills and the ability to challenge students' thinking—but who do not currently work with undergraduates in introductory and gateway courses—could be provided with appropriate incentives to do so. Senior faculty also could serve as role models to the more junior faculty who may be involved in the teaching of these courses.

". . . In reality, however, the undergraduate in our time may have little or no direct contact with established scholar-teachers. Instruction very often comes through the scholar's apprentice, the graduate student; the academic luminary featured in admissions bulletins appears rarely if at all in undergraduate classes, and then too often as the lecturer addressing hundreds of students at once. The context is intimidating for many, and they turn away in discouragement. Recognizing that discouragement, some research universities have responded by instituting smaller classes (though usually only for majors) conducted by senior faculty, or undergraduate seminars in which senior students are challenged to produce their own research."

Boyer Commission on Educating Undergraduates in the Research University, 1998, pg. 16

---

6. Establishing reward incentives for faculty and departments to contribute to the sustained availability of interdepartmental, integrative courses and excellence in teaching.

Individual faculty or single departments may develop innovative courses and programs, but such initiatives most likely will be sustained if a critical mass of faculty members and departments is involved. When other faculty not involved in the original innovation are able to reap the benefits of such change, innovation can be sustained. When these innovations become ingrained in the fabric of the curriculum, disciplinary departments will have incentives to participate and even expand innovation (see also Discussion and Recommendations for **Vision 4**).

Deans may want to provide financial and other resources and incentives to departments and faculty so that the costs of developing and maintaining exemplary introductory courses, including committed personnel, are not borne directly by the departments that are the principal participants. Such incentives could include supplementary budgets to individual departments for multi-disciplinary courses that involve more than one science department. Budgets could take into account student enrollments.

7. Providing avenues for students, alumni, professional advisory groups, and the community to participate in the development of new, interdisciplinary courses.

Too often, a key ingredient missing from course development and curriculum design is input from the students about their interests and needs (Benjamin and Carroll, 1993; Oblinger, 1995). It would be valuable if administrative staff, with the help of faculty, asked incoming and upper-division students to articulate the kinds of topics that should be addressed in these introductory courses. Alumni, local businesses, industries, and not-for-profit organizations also could be asked to provide feedback and comments. College committees that consider proposals and distribute funds for course development could ask current students and alumni who work in a variety of fields to serve as reviewers of these proposals. Involvement by different segments of the community, especially by those who would benefit directly, could enable faculty to develop and implement such courses more efficiently. The community approach also could result in the use of many interesting, timely, and relevant topics for these courses that are of particular appeal to a broad range of students.

8. Encouraging faculty to interact with partners both across campus and at other nearby two- and four-year institutions to share effective teaching practices and course and curricular innovations.

Such dissemination could be undertaken through the campus Teaching and Learning Center, in periodic staff newsletters, or by publishing the proposals and final reports from faculty who receive funds for course improvements and innovations. Honorary awards could be established for effective teaching that would require recipients to discuss their innovations with the larger campus community.

9. Including the space needs of lower-division teaching in active learning environments and of undergraduate research participation when planning for capital improvement projects and allocating resources.

Many colleges and universities envision in traditional ways the space and time required for introductory and lower-division courses. For example, traditional classrooms or large lecture halls are the typical settings. Laboratory sections are taught in three- or four-hour blocks of time. This view of introductory courses makes designing facilities and allocating resources for such courses a relatively straightforward exercise.

In contrast, active learning environments can place new demands on the design and use of facilities and equipment and the allocation of resources: simply stated, the traditional may not work. In the traditional classroom space, for example, immovable chairs and other furniture may discourage the kinds of discussion and interactions among students and faculty that encourage active teaching and learning. In traditional teaching laboratories, peninsula benches with utility conduits running down the center of the bench may serve as physical and psychological barriers to students who need to work in teams and share data or instrumentation.

If undergraduates are to study and experience SME&T as if they were practicing scientists and engineers, recognition also is needed of the fact that scientists and engineers typically do not conduct and complete their research projects in specific blocks of time. Students who are actively engaged in inquiry-based projects may need to be in the laboratory at times other than when their laboratory sections are scheduled. In these cases, additional or reallocated resources will be needed to cover the costs of laboratory supervision and security during evenings and weekends. If students in these courses must rely on information technology to complete their work, then assistance must be easily accessible for the technical problems that invariably arise.

Narum (1995) discusses planning new or renovating existing facilities to accommodate such changes in curriculum and work habits of students. Additional consideration of this issue also can be found under **Vision 5** in this report beginning on page 48.

Individual faculty and academic departments can implement Vision 2 by

1. Working with colleagues who teach introductory interdisciplinary courses to delineate carefully fundamental concepts about the natural and human-constructed world to which students should be exposed.

Regardless of the theme or topic of the course, the common themes might include (e.g., see Moore, 1995):

- *The scientific and engineering method:* What are the processes that scientists use to investigate a problem? What kinds of questions do scientists and engineers ask when trying to solve problems? How are these approaches similar to and different from each other? What are hypotheses? Theories? Controls? Variables? How do these terms, as used by scientists, mathematicians, and engineers differ from their colloquial usage?

- *Evidence and proof:* Why are some theories considered by most scientists as equivalent to fact (e.g., evolution) when they are so hotly disputed outside of science? What kind of evidence is required for scientists to accept a scientific theory? How are alternative or competing theories evaluated? What are the roles of intuition and the "discovery" approach in moving science and technology forward? Do scientists always display objectivity when addressing scientific questions or issues?

- *Science as a "way of knowing" and the limits to such knowledge:* How are the approaches that scientists employ to view and understand the universe similar to, and different from, the approaches taken by scholars in other disciplines outside of the natural sciences? What kinds of questions can be answered by the scientific and engineering methods, and what kinds of questions lie outside of these realms of knowledge? How does one distinguish between science and pseudoscience? Why are scientists often unable to provide definitive answers to questions they investigate? What are risk and probability, and what roles do they play when one is trying to provide scientific answers to questions? What is the difference between correlation and causation?

- *The relationships among basic science, applied science, and technology:* What are the realms and limits of basic science, applied science, and technology? How are basic science, applied science, and technology related to and dependent upon one other (e.g., Hurd, 1994)? In what ways are the questions that engineers ask similar to and different from those asked by natural scientists? How is scientific research conducted and supported in the United States?

- *The connections between the natural and mathematical sciences:* In what ways are mathematical and statistical concepts used by scientists to develop and test hypotheses, to analyze data, to reach conclusions, and to make further predictions? How have discoveries in mathematics led to new insights in science (e.g., fractal geometry, chaos theory, game theory) and technology? How can non-scientist citizens use these methods to evaluate scientific issues of importance to them and their communities?

- *The relationship, relevance, and importance of science to other fields of knowledge and to society:* How have science and technology influenced the history and social structure of human society? How have other intellectual disciplines (e.g., philosophy) and the social milieu in which science and technology are conducted influenced the kinds of scientific and engineering questions asked and the type of research undertaken?

- *Scientific conduct and ethics:* Are there any kinds of experiments that should not be performed or inventions that should not be produced? Who should decide? How have different branches of the natural sciences and engineering, individually and collectively, contributed to general knowledge and policy decisions related to personal and community health, industrial practices, and other societal issues? How has society affected the conduct and progress of science and technology?

2. Devising a plan for involving all undergraduates in at least one laboratory experience, including—for all interested SME&T majors—an experience in supervised original research, on- or off-campus, for at least one academic term.

Learning about SME&T in classrooms, especially in large lecture sections, can be an abstract and passive experience for many students. In contrast, students often report that SME&T comes alive for them when they are given the opportunity to work as scientists and engineers do, posing original questions, designing ways to answer those questions, and analyzing whether their original hypotheses are valid (McNeal and D'Avanzo, 1997).

Unfortunately, this discovery approach to learning through research is unavailable to vast numbers of undergraduates. Although comprehensive data are not available, anecdotal information indicates a reverse trend: a reduction in the number and even elimination of labs offered with lower-division courses because of fiscal constraints (Joan Prival,

National Science Foundation, personal communication). This is true even for some of the nation's research-intensive universities (Boyer Commission on Educating Undergraduates in the Research University, 1998).

In institutions where laboratory experiences are required for all undergraduates, these experiences may only involve following rote procedures to address predetermined questions and to arrive at conclusions that are widely known and available through textbooks or other sources. Problems and issues that scientists and engineers face everyday, such as designing adequate controls, accounting for interacting variables, replicating findings, and dealing with the uncertainty of statistical analysis of data, often are not presented to students in introductory or lower-division SME&T courses. Students who do not continue their SME&T studies stand a good chance never to appreciate fully how scientific investigations are conducted or how the concepts and facts that they have studied were generated. Every undergraduate should experience the logic, joy, and frustration of asking original questions and carrying out a plan to address them.

3. Emphasizing the development of introductory SME&T courses that include applications and hands-on learning experiences.

Currently, many SME&T curricula require students to learn much of the fundamentals before being allowed to apply them. This approach has been documented as driving even strong students away from further studies in SME&T (Stalheim-Smith and Scharmann, 1994; Seymour and Hewitt, 1997). A powerful alternative is introductory SME&T courses that allow students to share in the excitement of applying the fundamentals of one or more of the scientific disciplines to a problem or issue. For example, there are freshman year design courses that allow students to "do" engineering by working in teams on real projects (e.g., National Research Council, 1995a; Drexel University's Engineering Curriculum; Carnegie Mellon University's

undergraduate program in engineering; Rensselaer Polytechnic Institute's Studio Physics Program; and Dickinson College's Project Physics Program[10]—as well as courses found in McNeal and D'Avanzo, 1997).

Further, the engineering community has recognized the value of this alternative approach. Indeed, beginning in the Year 2000, all engineering programs will be evaluated for accreditation using new outcomes-based standards developed by the Accreditation Board for Engineering and Technology (ABET). These standards call for accreditation based in part on evaluations of student progress; program educational objectives, outcomes, and assessments; facilities; and institutional support.[11]

4. Sharing course syllabi, examinations, assignments, and laboratory experiments and expectations, successes, and failures with departmental colleagues, other faculty members, and academic advisors whose students are taking innovative introductory SME&T courses.

Time could be set aside at department meetings for discussion of an innovative or proven course activity (with the understanding that sharing such information could be helpful, including for avoiding mistakes). Colleagues from other departments could be invited as well but primarily to discuss ways to provide better integration and connections in subject matter across disciplines. For example, faculty who teach the introductory courses in biology, physics, and chemistry might agree not only to present a topic that is common to all three subjects (e.g., aspects of energy) at a prearranged time during the

---

[10]More information about Drexel University's Engineering Curriculum is available at <http://wwwtdec.coe.drexel.edu/mTDEC/Title.html>

More information about Carnegie Mellon University's undergraduate engineering program is available at <http://www.cit.cmu.edu/undergrad/undergrad.html>

More information about Rensselaer Polytechnic Institute's Studio Physics Program is available at <http://www.rpi.edu/dept/phys/education.html>

More information about Dickinson College's Project Physics Program is available at <http://Physics.Dickinson.edu/>

[11]Additional information about these new standards is available at <http://www.abet.org/eac/eac2000.htm>

semester but also to make specific reference at that time in each course about how the topic is relevant to the other disciplines.

5. Adopting formal mechanisms whereby faculty in different departments who teach similar concepts can share information about what is being learned in innovative courses, including the use of effective techniques and materials.

One such mechanism would arise naturally if faculty and departments worked together to develop and teach courses (especially those with a multidisciplinary or interdisciplinary focus). In such a case, individual faculty could then rotate responsibilities for teaching among course developers and colleagues with similar interests. This also would permit courses similar in content but featuring different emphases to be offered regularly to students without burdening one department with the sole responsibility for planning and teaching these courses. For example, an introductory interdisciplinary course that focused on scientific perspectives of energy could rotate among departments of physics, chemistry, geology, and biology. Each department could emphasize its own discipline while offering students a broad perspective. Under such a scenario, faculty in each department would be expected to participate in the course, yet no individual faculty member and no one department would need to take full-time responsibility for it.

6. Encouraging faculty who were not original designers of an innovation to participate in the resulting courses without having to take full responsibility for teaching or maintaining them.

In original research, ideas and innovations are discussed and evaluated and then widely disseminated, but this is not often the case in education. Rather, new ideas and products in education are usually worked on by individual instructors behind office and classroom doors (e.g., Shulman, 1993). Consequently, the longevity of many truly innovative courses often is the length of time their creators

teach them. Because few formal or widely recognized mechanisms currently exist for distributing what the creator has learned and produced,[12] colleagues across campus or even down the hall in the same department may be completely unaware of innovations that could inform their own teaching or serve as the basis for collaboration.

A recent study of college and university departments demonstrated that such innovation sharing could heighten efficacy. In the study, the departments recognized as most highly effective were those where faculty regularly shared knowledge and insights about courses, student learning, and pedagogy and considered such activities to be an integral component of their mission (e.g., National Research Council, 1991; Wergin, 1994).

7. Discussing curricular as well as non-curricular issues (e.g., use and sharing of facilities and equipment) with everyone involved with an interdisciplinary course.

Interdisciplinary courses often are taught with colleagues who may have very different ideas about course objectives, outcomes, content, and perspective. Also, facilities and instrumentation may be needed for such courses that lie outside of an individual faculty member's purview or control. Discussion among all of the stakeholders for the intended course is necessary, therefore. Such discussion can be expected to focus on tools, space requirements, and "territorial barriers," but it should also involve the defining of values,

---

[12]Some organizations concerned with improving undergraduate SME&T have begun to make such materials available via the Internet. For example, Project Kaleidoscope <http:/www.pkal.org>, Howard Hughes Medical Institute <http://www.hhmi.org>, National Engineering Education Delivery System (NEEDS) <http://fisc.berkeley.edu:7521/articles/ims-seminar-980817/BrandonMuramatsu/sld003.htm>, the Coalition for Education in the Life Sciences <http://www.wisc.edu/cels>, and others all have established databases that offer users information about courses, teaching techniques, and other pedagogical issues. The National Science Foundation also is beginning to assess whether it should support a digital National Library for undergraduate SME&T education that would offer users an interactive means for locating vast sources of information, published literature, and other materials from all realms of the sciences, mathematics, engineering, and technology (National Research Council, 1998a; see also <http://www.nap.edu/readingroom/enter2.cgi?ED.html>).

content, and pedagogy (see also additional discussion of this topic in **Vision 3**, Strategy 3, beginning on page 39). It should include recognition that many "best practices" in education are not limited by lack of technology or resources and, if necessary, faculty should be encouraged to begin with "pencil-and-paper" innovations and then move to more resource intensive methods where warranted.

8. Offering local workshops, possibly seeking the advice of outside experts from other two- and four-year institutions, on innovations that foster undergraduate learning.

Departments need not depend solely on their own resources to keep abreast of educational innovations for undergraduates. Outside speakers could be invited to give departmental, divisional, and institution-wide lectures, demonstrations, or seminars. Colleagues from other departments or institutions with expertise in pedagogy and learning could be invited to give presentations during department meetings on topics of interest. Educational research as well as innovative course design could be the subjects addressed. At departmental research seminars and colloquia, the speaker's teaching responsibilities and experience could be emphasized during introductions.

*See Appendix A for additional information about and strategies for implementation of **Vision 2** as discussed during the Committee on Undergraduate Science Education's "Year of Dialogue" regional symposia and topical forums.*

VISION 3

All colleges and universities would continually and systematically evaluate the efficacy of courses in SME&T.

Faculty would continually evaluate their courses for efficacy in promoting student

learning. Such evaluations would reflect in part the emphases outlined for **Vision 2**. Thus, in addition to mastery of the specific subject matter taught in a course, success also would be defined and measured by the degree of understanding and appreciation gained by students of both general scientific concepts and of the scientific approach to understanding natural processes. Evaluations would include measurements of learning at several levels: in the courses themselves, in subsequent SME&T courses, and, ultimately, in career and life. The results of such evaluations would be used continually to produce improvements in courses for students both inside and outside of the major, to assist in the professional development of individual faculty, and to allow departments continually to assess and improve their curricular offerings.

Background

Some innovations in undergraduate SME&T education have been spurred by recent calls for reform. However, it is not yet clear whether these innovations have made any difference in the number and types of students who enroll and are retained in SME&T courses and programs or in levels of scientific literacy. There simply has been too little effort to measure objectively, using established experimental protocols and statistical tools, changes in learning outcomes for students. Just as scholars are expected to incorporate into their research experimental designs that can be statistically analyzed, so too planning for courses should include ways to measure efficacy along pre-established parameters.

Similarly, just as the results of SME&T research are published and widely disseminated, so too should be examples of particularly effective SME&T courses, course or laboratory modules, and experiments on the improvement of teaching and learning. Means of dissemination should include presentations at professional meetings and publication in refereed journals. In the future, additional avenues for disseminating such work may become available through digital libraries that are established for this purpose (e.g., National Research Council, 1998a).

In addition to evaluations of courses or course materials, there should be an evaluation of faculty members' teaching abilities. Students, faculty peers, and supervisors could conduct such evaluations. Although student and faculty peer evaluations are common, many scholars and organizations are working to resolve the outstanding issues, including problems of subjectivity that could be inherent in these instruments (e.g., Centra et al., 1987; Hutchings, 1996; England et al., 1996; Glassick et al., 1997; Williams and Ceci, 1997). Several alternative assessment and evaluation tools and techniques are also being tested at increasing numbers of postsecondary institutions (Edgerton et al, 1991; Anderson, 1993; Diamond and Adam, 1993), and at least one website has been established by the National Institute for Science Education at the University of Wisconsin (NISE) to provide field-tested learning assessment guides (see <http://newtraditions.chem. wisc.edu/ FLAG/nt-flag.htm>).

If systemic improvements are to be made in undergraduate SME&T education, ways must be found to articulate what those improvements should be and to observe, record, and analyze whether they have actually taken place. Information about effective courses should be shared with the SME&T community, and effective teaching should be recognized and rewarded in personnel decisions.

Strategies for Promoting and Implementing Vision 3

Executive and academic officers of postsecondary institutions can implement Vision 3 by

1. Benchmarking undergraduate programs within their institutions against the best practices of peer institutions.

Comparing the quality and success of teaching across different departments within an institution and even across courses in a department has been problematic in higher education. Attempting to undertake such comparisons across institutions would seem nearly impossible. However, regional or statewide consortia of similar types of colleges and universities could enable departments and programs at specific postsecondary institutions to compare their educational objectives and their courses and programs with others in the state or region. Nationally, higher education organizations that represent particular types of postsecondary institutions (e.g., research universities, two-year colleges) could establish task forces to gather and disseminate information about innovative and demonstrably effective practices at member institutions.[13] For example, these organizations could facilitate dissemination of information about courses and programs as well as mechanisms employed by individual institutions to evaluate those courses and programs via the Internet. This type of effort could have far-reaching and long-lasting impacts on students and faculty in the nation's colleges and universities.

2. Requiring that any proposal submitted to the institution that seeks funds to create new courses, to modify existing courses, or to explore some alternative approach to teaching SME&T courses contain information about how the course or teaching practice will be evaluated for effectiveness.

By requiring a detailed plan for evaluating the efficacy of a research project, granting agencies compel applicants to think seriously about outcomes of their projects beyond the data that are generated and analyzed. Designing new courses, modifying existing courses, or embarking on an alternative path

---

[13]For example, in 1998, the Presidents of the Association of American Universities (AAU) commissioned a task force to examine current practices among member institutions and to offer recommendations for improving undergraduate education at these institutions with regard to admissions policies, introductory courses, and teacher preparation.

to teaching similarly should be viewed by both applicant faculty and awarding institutions as serious scholarly activities worthy of serious evaluation (Boyer, 1990; Glassick et al., 1997). Applications should contain evaluation plans as an integral component of the project to be funded.

3. Encouraging participation in departmental assessments as a significant component of individual faculty evaluations for promotion, tenure, and post-tenure review.

Departments in which faculty play an active role in collectively planning their course offerings and curriculum, in discussing teaching and learning issues, and in continually monitoring and evaluating their programs are viewed both by students and institutional colleagues as being strong and vital (Massy et al., 1994; Wergin, 1994; Hutchings, 1996). If faculty are to embrace the evaluation and ongoing quality of a department's educational programs as fundamental components of their professional responsibilities, the institution and its leaders should clearly communicate their expectations to all continuing faculty members. Faculty participation in the monitoring and improvement of departmental offerings also should be considered favorably in personnel decisions and appropriately rewarded.

Individual faculty and academic departments can implement Vision 3 by

1. Setting clear learning goals for individual courses and for the department's curriculum in general, especially for introductory and general education courses that the department oversees.

These goals should articulate learning outcomes for students (what students know, understand, and are able to do). Learning outcomes also might include how the course or curriculum has been structured to meet the needs of students with diverse backgrounds and interests (e.g., students planning to major in the discipline, students taking

these courses as requirements for other majors and programs, and students seeking to become teachers). In addition, courses might be assessed for evidence of how well they serve as gateways to higher level study.

Finally, because there may be high attrition in SME&T courses by motivated and capable students (e.g., Seymour and Hewitt, 1997), departments and institutions should continually monitor and access dropout and failure rates in these courses, especially at the introductory level. If these rates are found to be excessive, departments should investigate the cause or causes and work to correct the problem.

2. Including both undergraduate and graduate student representatives in departmental discussions about individual courses and/or curricular issues.

Students who are asked to assume such responsibilities usually take them seriously and often provide insights and "reality checks" to both faculty and departments about individual courses and/or curricula.

3. Involving departmental colleagues in substantive, regular evaluation of teaching and curriculum.

While there are many possible avenues for evaluation, it is important for department members to commit to working with each other to improve teaching and learning and to introduce continual innovation into the curriculum. This may require consideration of the use of innovative evaluation instruments. In addition to measuring specific content knowledge, innovative evaluation instruments should measure such skills as applying course content to solving problems, analyzing data, developing hypotheses, and the other types of skills and knowledge that are described on pages 33 through 34.

4. Providing active learning environments for all students, even in large section, lecture-dominated courses.

SME&T faculty and departments should place greater emphasis in their courses on inquiry-based projects through laboratory and field experiences and small discussion groups. Sources of relevant information include scholarly journals that feature innovative, effective teaching in SME&T (e.g., various disciplinary journals and journals such as the *Journal of College Science Teaching*). In addition, several recent publications (and at least one website) offer specific suggestions for implementing such alternative methods for undergraduate teaching as well as examples of successful programs. Four of these recently available resources are described below:

- *Science Teaching Reconsidered: A Handbook* (National Research Council, 1997a[14]), authored by the Committee on Undergraduate Science Education, provides many suggestions for improving the teaching of science for undergraduates who are and are not majoring in science. It draws on the results of education research and the experiences of successful science faculty members. Practical guidelines for experimenting with alternative pedagogies and a long list of references for further study are provided.

- *Handbook on Teaching Undergraduate Science Courses: A Survival Training Manual* (Uno, 1997[15]) focuses on problems that new faculty, especially those in the biological sciences, might face during their first years as faculty members. Many ideas about how to become an effective and engaging teacher who can offer courses that encourage students to "learn about, participate, and appreciate science and biology" (p. 1) are offered. The handbook also serves to introduce new science faculty to educational research and provides critical references.

- *Student-Active Science: Models of Innovation in College Science Teaching* (McNeal and D'Avanzo, 1997) is the result a National Science Foundation-sponsored conference held in 1996 entitled "Inquiry Approaches to Science Teaching." Through a series of papers, *Student-Active Science* provides a history of the current emphasis on "hands-on active education." Case studies are used to describe how a variety of postsecondary institutions have revised their curricula in the life sciences, chemistry, mathematics, and physics. *Student-Active Science* also describes different approaches to interdisciplinary courses and programs and ways to assess and evaluate innovations.

- *Peer Instruction: A User's Manual* (Mazur, 1997). Harvard University physics professor Eric Mazur's manual provides details of implementing "peer instruction" in large lectures. Essentially, within a lecture-based course, physics concepts are divided into discrete, short lectures. After each short lecture, students discuss the concept involved with their neighbors to enable them to explain and comprehend the concept more fully. Incorporating this style into traditional lectures requires little effort and no additional funds, according to Mazur.[16]

- In addition, the National Institute for Science Education (NISE) has established a worldwide website that focuses on collaborative learning (<http://www.wcer.wisc.edu/nise>).

5. Hiring within SME&T departments individuals who wish to pursue research on how undergraduate students learn.

By hiring scholars with expertise in SME&T education research and recognizing their research as equivalent to that undertaken by other department members, SME&T departments can send powerful messages to current college faculty, future K-12 teachers, and graduate and postdoctoral fellows about the importance of improving teaching and

---

[14]Also available electronically from the National Academy Press at < http://www.nap.edu>

[15]Available on the World Wide Web at <http://www.ou.edu/cas/botany-micro/faculty/uno-book.shtml>

[16]Additional information is available at <http://mazur-www.harvard.edu/Education/PI.html>

learning. SME&T faculty and education faculty could co-advise graduate students who are undertaking research in SME&T undergraduate education. Faculty members in SME&T departments could pursue research in teaching and learning in their discipline as the primary focus of their scholarship, or as a component. Joint appointments could be made both to an academic department and the institution's school of education. Research opportunities also could be provided to current and future teachers. Such opportunities would provide pre-service teachers with invaluable experiences and would help dispel myths about the research capabilities of teachers in education and in SME&T disciplines.

See Appendix A for additional information about and strategies for implementation of **Vision 3** *as discussed during the Committee on Undergraduate Science Education's "Year of Dialogue" regional symposia and topical forums.*

VISION 4

SME&T faculties would assume greater responsibility for the pre-service and in-service education of K-12 teachers.

Improving the SME&T education of both pre-service and in-service K-12 teachers is one of the most important challenges facing college and university faculties.[17] Scientists, mathematicians, engineers, and teacher educators all need to share responsibility for teacher preparation (e.g., Riley, 1998). If **Vision 4** were to be realized, these faculty would provide integrated pre-service and in-service experiences that blend scientific knowledge with pedagogical methods and effective teaching practices. Teacher education programs would

be informed by the *National Science Education Standards* (National Research Council, 1996b), the *Curriculum and Evaluation Standards for School Mathematics* and the *Professional Development Standards for Teaching Mathematics* (National Council of Teachers of Mathematics, 1989, 1991), the *Standards for Technology Education* (The International Technology Education Association, in preparation[18]), and other national and state-level science and mathematics education reform initiatives (e.g., American Association for the Advancement of Science, 1993; Council of Chief State School Officers, 1997).

A critical component of new teacher preparation programs would be the adoption of teaching approaches that enhance pre-service teachers' desire to continue both their professional development and their own personal learning. Science faculty need to become involved in this effort by providing motivating pre-service and in-service opportunities for scientific discovery for K-12 science educators in the classroom, in laboratories, and in the field. Pre-service opportunities also could include classroom teachers and scientists working together with students through school/college partnerships.

Background

Pre-service Education

The growth of standards-based education in grades K-12 requires not only the education and certification of greater numbers of science and mathematics teachers but also a different paradigm for their pre-service education. Given the new standards, most K-4 teachers will now need a general education in the sciences and mathematics and the skills

---

[17]For a more in-depth study of this topic, see the National Commission on Teaching and America's Future's reports entitled *What Matters Most: Teaching for America's Future* and *Doing What Matters Most: Investing in Quality Teaching*. These two important reports explain the challenges of preparing future teachers and offer findings and recommendations for improvement.

[18]The *Standards for Technology Education* are expected to be released in the spring of 1999. CUSE members have not reviewed the standards but know that the authoring committee, the International Technology Education Association (ITEA), has modeled its efforts on the standards work of the National Council of Teachers of Mathematics and the National Research Council. Indeed, several members of these earlier standards efforts are members of the ITEA working group.

> "It has become impossible to ignore the mounting evidence that our elementary and secondary public schools are not performing as they should. Some say we have a national crisis on our hands. Although we in higher education are very skillful at ignoring the obvious, it is gradually dawning on some of us that we bear a substantial part of the responsibility for this sad situation and, hence, and [sic] equally substantial responsibility for dealing with it. Moreover, it is increasingly clear that our role must extend far beyond helping out embattled K-12 colleagues with 'their' problems. We need to deal with our own, including the way we educate and train the teachers and administrators of the K-12 schools, as well as the processes by which high-school graduates become college students and graduates. Simply put, pervasive K-12 reform requires—and cannot succeed without—higher education reform. That is, we must have K-16 reform!"
>
> ***Langenberg, 1997, pg. 1***

to engage students in exploration of the natural world, especially as encountered in their own communities. Middle-school teachers of science and mathematics (grades 5 to 8) will now need broader knowledge of these disciplines and the skills to help their students engage in meaningful scientific inquiry. And high-school science teachers will need to have a deep knowledge of the scientific or mathematical disciplines they teach and detailed knowledge of the strengths and limitations of the scientific method. High-school teachers also will need to be equipped to help students understand that science is a "way of knowing" that can be compared with other ways of knowing (Moore, 1993).

If teachers "teach as they are taught," it is then imperative that we improve the undergraduate SME&T education of *all* future teachers, not just those who will become science or mathematics specialists. Several documents and reports have been published or are now in preparation to help teachers, schools, and

school systems use national standards-based instruction and instructional materials in the classroom (e.g., National Research Council, 1997c; National Science Teachers Association's Scope, Sequence and Coordination Project[19]) and to guide postsecondary institutions in preparing teachers before and during service to be able to teach a standards-based curriculum (e.g., National Council of Teachers of Mathematics, 1991; Diez et al., 1993; National Research Council, 1996c, 1996d, 1997b, 1997d; National Science Foundation, 1993, 1996b). For example, the *National Science Education Standards* emphasize the responsibilities of postsecondary institutions in preparing all future teachers (those who are and are not science specialists) and in providing continuing opportunities for professional development to all practicing teachers (National Research Council, 1996b). This emphasis can be found in the recommendations and calls for action by many in the science and mathematics community (e.g., McDermott, 1990; Leitzel, 1991; National Science Foundation, 1993, 1996b; Kirwan, 1994; National Research Council, 1996c, 1996d; Watson, 1998).

Most of the organizations and researchers committed to the improvement of teacher education in SME&T agree that essential steps include the lowering of departmental, institutional, and collegial barriers and far greater professional contact between faculty in SME&T departments and in schools of education. For example, the American Physical Society's (APS) Committee on Education is responsible for initiatives and activities that "improve the cooperation between the educational community and other parts of the physics community."[20] Similarly, for many years, the American Association of Physics Teachers (AAPT) has sponsored programs that encourage college and university faculty in physics to work

---

[19]Available on the World Wide Web at <http://www.gsh.org/NSTA_SSandC/>

[20]Additional information is available on line at <http://www.aps. org/educ/coe/coe.htm>

with their high-school counterparts to improve physics teaching at all levels. AAPT's Committee on Research in Physics Education examines and disseminates the results of research about how students learn physics and how that knowledge can be used to improve classroom instruction.[21] The American Society for Microbiology's Board on Education and Training identifies its constituencies as "educators in all fields."[22] *All* faculty, regardless of discipline, should recognize their mutual role as educators of future disciplinary experts and future K-12 teachers (National Research Council, 1997b).

Despite the fact that some professional societies have long histories of promoting connections between the K-12 and higher education communities within their disciplines, several factors have contributed to the current low or nonexistent level of interaction between SME&T faculty and colleagues in schools of education at many postsecondary institutions. These factors include the trend in modern American colleges and universities toward overspecialization in specific disciplines that has produced too little contact between faculty in different departments and nearly none focusing on teachers. Institutional organizational structures that have evolved in part due to federal policies in support of research have intensified the disciplinary affiliation of faculty members on many campuses. In addition, the faculty reward structure has intensified the dominance of disciplinary interests over a more collegial-based system of values, rewards, and recognition (Boyer, 1990; Glassick et al., 1997; Boyer Commission on Educating Undergraduates in the Research University, 1998).

As a consequence of these factors, SME&T faculty typically are not well informed about current research on how students learn and how science and mathematics can be taught more effectively (e.g., Gabel, 1994). In some cases, these faculty may not even realize that an extensive body of research-based information exists on these subjects. Similarly, faculty in colleges and schools of education typically are not well informed about the current scientific research, particularly in emerging areas.

In addition, although the education and mentoring of pre-service teachers is optimized when professionals in schools of education, faculty in SME&T departments, and master teachers from the local community work together (e.g., Darling-Hammond, 1997), such cooperation is rare. Many education and SME&T faculty are removed from exposure to teachers in the classroom. Faculty in schools of education often have little direct interaction with K-12 science teachers, even at local schools. SME&T faculty may never see or work with pre-service teachers outside of their courses, if then.

"Lack of interaction among SME&T faculty, faculty in other academic disciplines, and faculty in schools of education is a serious flaw in much of pre-college teacher preparation, arising in a separation of methods from content."

National Science Foundation, 1996b, pg. 49

If the preparation of future science and mathematics teachers is to be aligned with calls from across the nation for standards-based education reform, *all* faculty, along with local schools, must work together fully to integrate content in subject areas and pedagogy (Bell and Buccino, 1997; see also National Science Foundation, 1998c, and U.S. Department of Education, 1998b, for examples of teacher education programs that involve both SME&T departments and schools of education). Future teachers cannot be expected to guide student learning in ways outlined in the *National Science Education Standards*, the National Council of Teachers of Mathematics K-12 standards, or

---

[21]Additional information is available on line at <http://www.aapt.org>

[22]Additional information is available at <http://www.asm.org/edusrc/edu7.htm>

"Scientists have an obligation to assist in science teachers' professional development. Many scientists recognize the obligation and are ready to get involved. Scientists can provide opportunities for teachers to learn how the scientific process works, what scientists do and how and why they do it. They can provide research opportunities for practicing teachers; act as scientific partners; provide connections to the rest of the scientific community; assist in writing grant proposals for science-education projects; provide hands-on, inquiry-based workshops for area teachers; and provide teachers access to equipment, scientific journals, and catalogs not usually available in schools. They can help teachers to review educational material for its accuracy and utility.

When scientists teach their undergraduate classes and laboratories, potential science teachers are present. Scientists should recognize that as an opportunity to promote and act as a model of both good process and accurate content teaching and so strive to improve their own teaching."

National Research Council, 1996d, pg. 3

---

state curriculum frameworks if they themselves have not experienced such pedagogical approaches in their own undergraduate SME&T courses. They must be exposed to such techniques and must be asked to think deeply about appropriate content across disciplines as outlined in **Vision 2**, Strategy 1 for faculty and academic departments (see pgs. 33 to 34).

In-service Education[23]

The knowledge base in virtually all fields of SME&T is increasing or is being revised with breathtaking rapidity. With the explosive

growth of the Internet, information about new developments and breaking events around the world and beyond is available almost instantaneously. Paradigms that served past generations of teachers for acquiring new knowledge, for locating existing information, and for critically evaluating the validity of available data are increasingly inadequate. In addition, expectations are changing about how to present subject matter to students. As standards-based reforms take hold, practicing teachers will need to revise fundamentally not only what but also how they teach their students. Regardless of the grade they teach, teachers cannot be effective in helping students learn about, understand, and appreciate science, mathematics, and technology if they themselves have not been exposed to and asked to think deeply about appropriate content within and across disciplines. Text beginning on pg. 33 under **Vision 2**, Strategy 1 for faculty and academic departments, provide examples of the kinds of thinking about SME&T to which practicing and prospective teachers should be exposed.

Although in-service programs within K-12 school systems can assist teachers in addressing content and teaching methodology issues, these programs too often fail to impart the deep understanding of content needed to sustain a long-term, systemic change in K-12 education. Teachers need ongoing opportunities to be lifelong learners and to keep abreast of recent developments in many fields, not only in the interest of staying current for their students but for remaining intellectually engaged for themselves. In addition, if teachers had such opportunities, the excitement that they experience would be imparted to their students. Many professions routinely provide opportunities for personal enrichment, for increasing professional skills and knowledge, and for interacting with others in the field: as professionals, teachers need and deserve these same opportunities.

---

[23]Some educators prefer to use the term "professional development" rather than "in-service" education. In-service education implies a top-down approach, in which college and university faculty or other service providers are the primary sources of knowledge and expertise. By contrast, professional development is an approach that emphasizes full partnership between K-12

and postsecondary faculty in professional communities that are dedicated to improving SME&T education (National Research Council, 1996d). The term "in-service" is used here because it is more familiar to many postsecondary faculty and administrators, but in this report—as in the National Research Council (1996d) report—professional development is the goal.

All colleges and universities need to consider the professional development of local teachers to be part of their educational mission. This mission could be accomplished through both formal and informal means. Formal course work offered to practicing teachers in SME&T should be rich in both content and pedagogy as outlined in the mathematics standards published by the National Council of Teachers of Mathematics and the *National Science Education Standards*.

Faculty in postsecondary institutions also could establish more collegial relations with their K-12 colleagues. Outreach programs could provide teachers with access to university library collections (both printed and electronic); invitations to lectures and other activities by visiting scholars; equipment that their schools cannot afford to purchase; and ongoing professional contacts with university scientists, mathematicians, and engineers. The cost to postsecondary institutions would be minimal, but the impact on the professional development of teachers could be profound. In addition, many of these opportunities are easily provided through local partnerships or alliances with local school districts. A large body of literature provides specific suggestions for establishing and maintaining such programs (e.g., Atkin and Atkin, 1989; Ostwald, 1994; Thorsen, 1994; National Research Council, 1996d; Bell and Buccino, 1997).

Strategies for Promoting and Implementing Vision 4

Executive and academic officers of postsecondary institutions can implement Vision 4 by

1. Making available new tenure-track faculty positions for candidates with dual backgrounds in a SME&T discipline and in science education who are interested in promoting innovative and effective undergraduate learning.

These positions could be jointly appointed in an academic department and in the school of education or in one primary department. The provision of oversight and professional development by both departments would be critical as the candidate moved toward professional advancement within the institution.

2. Actively promoting partnerships, consortia, or outreach programs with local school districts to advance the professional development of teachers and to provide resources not otherwise available to local schools.

Extensive research has demonstrated that professional connections among teachers of the K-12 grades and faculty in colleges and universities are sustained and nurtured when the individuals involved view each other as partners. Each group can offer and benefit from the resources, examples of effective practices, and professional insights of the other. Many examples of effective K-12/university partnerships are available (e.g., Atkin and Atkin, 1989; National Research Council, 1990, 1996d; Ostwald, 1994; Thorsen, 1994; Bybee, 1998).

Sustaining partnerships requires a great deal of time and nurturing. At least one person on the postsecondary campus with appropriate credentials and qualifications should be designated and recognized by the community as the coordinator of the program and appropriately compensated for the work involved. If necessary, a new position should be created.

3. Removing institutional obstacles to department donations and continued servicing of high-quality equipment to local school districts.

Many school districts have a low or nonexistent budget with which to purchase new scientific equipment, especially for the lower grade levels. Departments in postsecondary institutions that are retiring equipment should be permitted not only to donate this equipment to local schools but also to help schools maintain it. Alternatively, given the importance of proper maintenance and calibration, particularly of sensitive instruments, donors may want to require the schools to assume this responsibility as part of their end of the partnership.

In addition, teachers need to know the purpose and operation of the donated equipment and its potential for improving learning. To address this need, graduate or undergraduate work-study students (as part of their financial aid packages) could be assigned to conduct workshops on the use of equipment, to be available to answer questions, to troubleshoot problems, or to work directly with teachers in their classrooms in using the donated equipment.

4. Establishing an institutional "hot line" telephone number or current events website to provide local teachers with information about departmental or campus-wide events involving SME&T speakers or other activities.

Often the most valuable resources that can be made available to teachers and their students by postsecondary institutions are those that cost little or nothing, such as invitations to hear outside speakers and other visitors to the campus who have valuable perspectives on advances in SME&T. Postsecondary partners could establish a pre-recorded "hot line" or a special website or use existing SME&T departmental websites to provide teachers with timely information about such opportunities. This sharing of resources would also promote greater collegiality between college and K-12 instructors.

5. Providing incentives for faculty from schools of education and SME&T departments to work together to develop both certification options for science majors and continuing education courses for teachers that specifically examine the NCTM's Professional Standards for Teaching Mathematics and Curriculum and Evaluation Standards for School Mathematics, the National Science Education Standards, Benchmarks for Science Literacy, Resources for Science Literacy, Standards for Technology Education (in preparation), and state curriculum frameworks and how these can be implemented at various grade levels.

National and state standards provide a vision and guidelines for what students should know and be able to do in mathematics, science, and technology at various grade levels, but they intentionally do not provide specific curricula. Although a number of organizations are currently developing guides for how to use standards (e.g., National Research Council, 1998b) or have provided curricular materials (e.g., Texley and Wild, 1996; Lowery, 1997; American Chemical Society, 1997; National Academy of Sciences, 1998; National Science Resources Center, 1998), translating the various standards into actual classroom practice remains a challenge that teachers of grades K-16 should undertake together. Through continuing education courses on standards for K-12 teachers, faculty from SME&T departments and schools of education could provide local K-12 teachers with guidance on integrating standards-based approaches to teaching and learning into their local school curricula. In some cases, preparation for such courses could serve to keep SME&T and education faculty current in this area.

6. Making available financial resources to hire local master teachers as adjunct faculty to work with faculty in both schools of education and SME&T departments on improving pre-service education and in assessing student learning.

Teachers with years of experience in the classroom have a keen eye for recognizing when students are and are not learning what is being taught. In many districts, teachers who have been designated as "master teachers" often have undergone additional training in pedagogical techniques, child development, and cognition. They have developed innovative ways to present concepts and ideas that many students find difficult to grasp. In addition, they are well aware of the issues and difficulties that new teachers will face. Thus, master teachers hired as advisors or consultants could provide invaluable perspective to postsecondary faculty in both SME&T departments and in schools of education on both the content and pedagogy of teacher preparation programs in SME&T.

Such relationships might involve postsecondary institutions reimbursing local school districts for the salaries and benefits of these teachers, allowing them to spend a sabbatical leave on campus. Alternatively, SME&T departments and schools of education might jointly offer graduate-level credit to master teachers seeking advanced degrees.

Individual faculty and academic departments can implement Vision 4 by

1. Measuring the effectiveness of each component of the pre-service curriculum in fostering innovative pedagogy and in exploring SME&T concepts.

Universities should undertake long-term studies of their graduates who have embarked on careers in teaching to assess the effects of both the education and SME&T components of the institution's pre-service programs. The emphasis should be on how well the K-12 students of these teachers are learning science and mathematics and on how the teachers' performance was affected by their postsecondary curricular experiences. Results from these studies could then be shown to and discussed with newly hired teachers, their former education and SME&T professors, and relevant school system administrators.

2. Inviting regional K-12 science and mathematics teachers to participate in on-campus seminars where recent scientific or pedagogical research is discussed.

These seminars might consider such topics as the appropriate use in classrooms of information technology and the Internet or ways for postsecondary and K-12 schools to cooperate in implementing science and mathematics standards. The seminars and similar activities could be sponsored by both schools of education and SME&T departments to increase understanding and awareness among a wider spectrum of educators.

3. Inviting master teachers to serve as adjunct faculty and colleagues in **both** schools of education and SME&T departments.

If content and pedagogy are to be truly integrated components of teacher preparation programs, then master teachers with recognized teaching skills and a great deal of experience in the classroom should become more directly involved with both the practicum and course work activities of pre-service teachers. These master teachers could be local teachers from different grade levels or from other local two- and four-year postsecondary institutions who have been recognized for their teaching prowess and accomplishments. They could be brought into two- and four-year college and university classrooms and laboratory settings as jointly appointed adjunct faculty. These master teachers would benefit not only the students who are future teachers but also the postsecondary faculty who are involved with the sponsoring institution's pre-service program. Pre-service teachers and postsecondary faculty could benefit both from gaining an understanding of the actual challenges that each of these groups of practicing master teachers faces and through direct exposure to effective teaching practice. Pre-service teachers could benefit from the opportunity to establish professional relationships with faculty from two- and four-year postsecondary institutions that could carry over to their induction years and beyond.

Master teachers of grades K-12 would benefit by being involved with such partnerships and working with community college and university colleagues. They could participate directly in or gain exposure to cutting-edge research and other opportunities to learn about new knowledge and controversies in established and emerging fields of SME&T. In addition, K-12 master teachers could participate in university-level courses, gain more direct access to visiting speakers and seminars for themselves and their students, and act as peer evaluators for assessing the teaching skills of their university colleagues. Finally, K-12 master teachers could benefit by learning techniques used in college-level SME&T teaching laboratories that might be useful for their own students.

4. Employing discipline-based science teachers in the continuing education of fellow teachers.

Teachers who have extensive training and background in science could be engaged to work with postsecondary faculty to provide courses and other in-service experiences for their fellow teachers. Such an approach might be particularly appropriate for professional development for the teachers of the primary and middle grades who often lack content knowledge but want more. This approach would have the added benefit of allowing teachers from different grade levels to interact much more than is usually possible during the school year and to discuss issues of common concern, such as coordination of curricula across grades and school levels.

See Appendix A for additional information about and strategies for implementation of **Vision 4** *as discussed during the Committee on Undergraduate Science Education's "Year of Dialogue" regional symposia and topical forums.*

VISION 5

All postsecondary institutions would provide the rewards and recognition, resources, tools, and infrastructure necessary to promote innovative and effective undergraduate SME&T teaching and learning.

The central importance of offering high-quality introductory SME&T courses must be visibly recognized through appropriate recognition of and rewards to individual faculty and staff and, collectively, to departmental and other program units. If **Vision 5** were to

be realized, postsecondary institutions would recognize and appropriately reward faculty leaders and departments or program units that have introduced new teaching and learning methods into their courses and curricular programs. Modern tools (e.g., access to information technology) and other kinds of institutional support would be provided to faculty and staff who wanted to use these tools in their classrooms and laboratories. Well-staffed resource centers would be provided where faculty and students could obtain the latest information about alternative and effective teaching and learning techniques. These resource centers also would serve as sites for piloting new programs and practicing effective teaching and assessment activities.

The authoring committee recognizes that implementing the visions of this report could require new funds or shifts in the allocation of resources. The costs involved may vary considerably from institution to institution. With the evidence and information provided in this report, the committee hopes to stimulate serious discussions at all higher education institutions that will take into account the need for new or reallocated resources to implement change.

Background

Rewards and Recognition

Because faculty time is the major resource required to fulfill the vision of high-quality introductory SME&T courses and curricula for all undergraduates, the reward and recognition system of academic departments and postsecondary institutions must be structured to encourage rather than discourage commitment of this time by faculty. Currently, two important barriers to change exist at many postsecondary institutions:

(1) Tenure and promotion depend on a faculty member's research, teaching, and service. However, some research universities place such a premium on research

that teaching performance often is perceived as having little more than a tie-breaking value in important personnel decisions, such as tenure, promotion, or merit salary increases (Boyer, 1990; Joint Policy Board for Mathematics, 1994; Kennedy, 1997; Boyer Commission on Educating Undergraduates in the Research University, 1998; however, see also Office of the President, University of California, 1991). Because some other postsecondary institutions are following the research university model, they are increasingly interested in the original research conducted by their faculty yet also continue to expect high levels of performance in teaching and service.

In two recent surveys, faculty and administrators at various institutions were asked about the direction their institutions *should* take with respect to emphasizing research, teaching, or some combination thereof. Results indicated that, between 1990 and 1992 and 1992 and 1994, faculty preference at institutions ranging in Carnegie categories from Research I to Baccalaureate II had shifted from a balanced emphasis to a stronger emphasis on teaching. Many of the respondents to the two surveys also indicated that while their institutions purported to emphasize a greater expectation for both teaching and research, the operative reward systems in their institutions did not support this emphasis (Gray et al., 1996).

(2) Faculty development of innovative courses for all students requires the interest and support of departments as well as the time and effort of the individual faculty members. However, pressures within the disciplines and departmental funding patterns strongly favor the recruitment and production of majors and future graduate students, not scientifically literate non-majors. Faculty need to see comparable incentives and rewards for teaching general education courses to students who will not go on to careers in SME&T. For such innovation to be sustained, departments must make it a priority to nurture the creativity of their individual faculty members and to disseminate the instructional and pedagogical fruits of their labors.

Resources, Tools, and Infrastructure

The absence of instructional resources, tools, and infrastructure support may limit or prevent course innovation. Two types of support are needed, as follows:

(1) **Support that integrates simulation and experimentation activities into the course (e.g., laboratory space, facilities and equipment for both 'wet' and 'dry' laboratory and field exercises).**

Collaborative learning and project-based learning often require ready access to information technology and networks as

---

"Rather than set arbitrary teaching loads for each faculty member, the dean or provost should enter into negotiations with a department to establish what its total obligation to undergraduate students is, including the vitally important individual contact such as advising and the supervision of independent study. In the course of the negotiations, the department would be forced to review and evaluate its curriculum, the kinds of educational opportunities it offers, and the engagement of individual faculty with different portions of the task. In the end, there would be a clear understanding of what the department is responsible for. For its part, the department would be able to meet those responsibilities in a flexible way, assigning the best lecturers to lower-division courses and the best small-group seminar leaders to courses of that kind . . . By making departments accountable for meeting well-defined obligations to students, the institution would also become more inclusive in its definition of what constitutes teaching."

Kennedy, 1997, pgs. 63-64

---

well as to classroom, laboratory, discussion, and study group spaces (e.g., Baker and Gifford, 1997; National Science Foundation, 1998b; Benson and Yuan, 1998). Such facilities should be available to students beyond regularly scheduled class times. The absence or limited availability of such space can be a major barrier on many campuses to implementing new approaches to teaching. New teaching and learning paradigms, such as collaborative learning teams, may also challenge existing college schedules and security arrangements or involve facilities that lie outside the physical boundaries of a department's classrooms and laboratory spaces. Institutions must find ways to make facilities more open while maintaining security and minimizing differences in departmental resources, physical space, and perceived "ownership" of resources by certain faculty or departments. Planning for supporting infrastructure does not need to precede planning for curriculum innovation. To the contrary, planning for new or reconstructed spaces and for new instrumentation and equipment is best undertaken *following* or *in conjunction* with the articulation of a plan about how those spaces and equipment would be used for teaching and learning (e.g., Narum, 1995).

(2) **Support that facilitates innovative approaches to computation, communication, and "visualization" of problems by students, among students, and between students and faculty.**

Such support would include ready access to the World Wide Web, publicly and commercially available databases, and computer hardware configured to run modern applications. Faculty and students also need "user-friendly" educational software that allows them to spend their time researching and solving problems generated by course work rather than troubleshooting software problems. However, faculty and their institutions must be careful to avoid equating ready accessibility to information technology and ease-of-use with quality teaching and learning. Preoccupation with tools rather than with teaching and learning processes may actually impede pedagogical and educational innovation (Ehrmann, 1995; National Science Foundation, 1998b).

Strategies for Promoting and Implementing Vision 5

Executive and academic officers of postsecondary institutions can implement Vision 5 by

1. Creating general and discipline-based Teaching and Learning Centers that
   - provide advice and technical support so that innovations can be implemented successfully;
   - provide students with internships, assistantships, or fellowships to encourage input into the development of courses; and
   - offer small grants to provide faculty with released time or other resources for particularly innovative SME&T course development that exceeds substantially the normal course preparation commitment.

Teaching and Learning Centers can provide expert staff and material resources to faculty at all levels to improve their classroom teaching and interactions with students as mentors and advisors. Academic officers should ensure that new or existing centers have both the staff expertise and resources to make readily available the latest information on SME&T education. These resources might include K-12 standards in science and mathematics as well as information about innovations in undergraduate SME&T education, especially new approaches for teaching within individual disciplines and in interdisciplinary SME&T courses. These resources and references could include those available through the Internet and in scholarly journals. Sustained support for such activities would most likely take place on campuses where faculty members were encouraged to use such centers and other resources as part of career-long professional development of their teaching skills and efficacy. Specialized support for the SME&T disciplines could be enhanced by staffing these centers with professionals who have specific backgrounds in SME&T, such as science librarians.

Another primary mission of Teaching and Learning Centers should be the dissemination of effective teaching tools and techniques. Center staff should recruit particularly effective teachers to serve as role models and speakers at campus discussions on teaching. Center staff could also make sure that the pedagogical techniques of these exemplars are recorded and disseminated to other colleagues on campus. In exchange for working with the Teaching and Learning Center to give presentations or record their innovations in writing or on videotape, these role models also could receive other forms of recognition, such as institutional stipends or access to student assistants to help with course development or research.

Many Teaching and Learning centers from a wide variety of postsecondary institutions now post information about their activities and available resources on the Internet. Because each center emphasizes different aspects of teaching and learning, it is difficult to characterize specific examples or models of successful centers. Readers are urged to explore the large number of websites now available from these centers. A listing of and pointers to Internet sites for a large number of Teaching and Learning Centers are available at <http://www.ukans.edu/~sypherh/bc/us.html>

2. Providing incentives, including recognition, to individual faculty to upgrade their teaching skills and knowledge of educational issues by participating in programs at their institution's Teaching and Learning Center and in departmental or cross-disciplinary seminars and workshops.

Individual faculty members typically teach in isolated classrooms and have little or no discussion with their colleagues concerning issues of teaching and learning. Unlike

their experiences in research, faculty members often lack opportunities to discuss theory, methods, and successes and failures in teaching. Faculty need to be encouraged to engage in such discussions, whether through formal programs or less formal seminars, as a means to encourage them and their departments to value teaching as a form of scholarship (Hutchings, 1996). A number of national organizations facilitate such communication by inviting faculty and administrative teams to participate in workshops or other activities related to teaching and learning.[24]

3. Providing incentives, including institutional recognition and additional financial support, to departments and other program units that collectively work to improve teaching, student learning, and curricular offerings to meet the needs of *all* of their students.

To encourage departments to work on improving undergraduate SME&T education as a unit, academic officers could provide some rewards or incentives to these units in addition to or perhaps even in place of those offered to individual faculty and staff. For example, some percentage of departmental budgets could reflect the implementation of one or another of the visions articulated in this report. Departments that do a particularly good job of implementing a vision could be recognized publicly, and their work could be publicized by the institution, both on-campus and externally (e.g., in local media or through alumni publications).

4. Making easily accessible to the faculty new software useful for common tasks, including those associated with innovative SME&T courses.

It is clear that when everyone in an institution uses the same operating system, word processing, spreadsheet, database, and World Wide Web browsing software, it is easier to focus more on work and less on the vagaries and nuances of the software. However, not

---

[24]For example, see activities of Project Kaleidoscope at <http://www.pkal.org>

every institution can or will standardize to this extent, in part due to the expense. At the very least, faculty should have easy access to new software that allows them to share data more easily and to experience fewer of the problems associated with converting formats. Non-faculty benefits would include less time spent by information technologies staff on learning how to fix new problems associated with exotic software applications and more time spent training other employees to use applications more effectively. Accordingly, it is important for the institution to provide sufficient access to both common information technology resources and web-based services for assigned work.

5. Devising a comprehensive plan to update or replace computer hardware, software, and associated resources on a regular basis.

As with most other disciplines, SME&T faculty, students, and departments increasingly depend on information from sources around the world to accomplish their work and to engage in the development of new courses and other projects. As the pace of innovation quickens in information technology, institutions of higher education must make conscious decisions to devote more of their resources to making sufficient numbers of appropriate and up-to-date tools available to teachers and learners. Regular replacement of the oldest hardware and software on campus and the transfer of previously purchased high-end equipment to users with less need for the latest innovation should become part of an overall institutional plan for providing everyone on campus with maximum needed access to information technology.

6. Working to assess and meet institution-wide needs for the space, equipment, and other resources needed to upgrade and improve the curriculum.

A comprehensive plan for curricular reform and innovation often points to the need to design new facilities or remodel old

ones. However, such a plan should not simply serve as a catalyst but also as a driver of the changes to be made. Academic leaders can assist the process by making clear to all involved that curriculum should drive the design of physical space. They can then work with individual faculty, departments, and programs to develop a vision for curricular innovation. Once the vision exists, it should be translated first into specific courses and activities and then into an identification of the kinds of space, instrumentation, and equipment needed to support these courses and activities. When all those steps have been taken, a comprehensive plan of action can be constructed and proposed to the community. Once the community has embraced the plan, campus leaders can approach potential donors for the needed funds.

Individual faculty and academic departments can implement Vision 5 by

1. Including a scholarly assessment of faculty participation in improving teaching and curriculum as one of the criteria for promotion, tenure, and other personnel decisions.

Many panels, commissions, and individual authors have addressed these issues (e.g., Boyer, 1990; Glassick et al., 1997; Kennedy, 1997). Some organizations have engaged colleges and universities in studies to find ways to incorporate comprehensive and fair assessment of teaching into personnel decisions (e.g., Hutchings, 1996). A detailed discussion of these issues is beyond the purview of this report. However, the authors of this report agree that if departments and institutions truly want faculty to view quality teaching of undergraduates as being on par with other scholarly responsibilities and achievements, they must require that clear evidence of such accomplishments be collected and submitted as part of all personnel decisions. In turn, institutions must provide clear evidence that this information will be considered as an integral part of their personnel decision-making process and that excellent teachers will be rewarded with the conferring of tenure or promotion in rank.

2. Using a departmental vision and plan for curricular innovation to guide requests for space and/or facilities utilization.

Because the curriculum should drive the design of space and/or facilities rather than the reverse, departments should be prepared to use their curricular vision and plans for innovation when issues regarding space and/or facilities arise (see Narum, 1995, and Strategy 4 on pg. 51).

3. Allocating space for students to work together in environments equipped with readily accessible research tools.

Undergraduates can benefit academically and intellectually by engaging in meaningful research problems both inside and outside of their regular course work (Project Kaleidoscope, 1991, 1994; Benson and Yuan, 1998). Such activities might require teamwork and be conducted in environments that provide ready access to computers and the Internet, for example.

4. Discussing case studies of innovative and effective practices in science and mathematics teaching as a routine part of departmental business.

Access to and discussion of case studies or teaching portfolios of faculty who have excelled in teaching or service (such as training K-12 teachers or working with industry) could be useful in helping other faculty to prepare their dossiers for tenure or promotion. Through exposure to these case studies, faculty could gain a broader understanding of the possible range of faculty contributions that might be considered in personnel decisions, for example. In addition, such discussions could help promote collegiality within departments as colleagues learn more about each other's contributions and promote greater equity among departments in the ways that faculty are evaluated for their

teaching accomplishments (Hutchings, 1993).

5. Discussing with colleagues information about effective teaching practices that is increasingly available on the World Wide Web.

The abundance of materials related to teaching and learning of SME&T subject matter on the World Wide Web offers new opportunities for faculty to learn from others in their disciplines around the world. Until this material is more systematically catalogued and reviewed for quality (e.g., National Research Council, 1998a), faculty members in a department can work with each other to share and discuss information about websites in their disciplines. Faculty also can urge their professional societies to collate and make this kind of information available on their websites and to share that information with other disciplines through website consortia. For example, the Council for Education in the Life Sciences now has a website that links users to the home pages of many professional societies in the biological sciences where information about biology teaching and learning can be easily accessed.[25]

Also see Appendix A for additional information about and strategies for implementation of **Vision 5** *as discussed during the Committee on Undergraduate Science Education's "Year of Dialogue" regional symposia and topical forums.*

VISION 6

Postsecondary institutions would provide quality experiences that encourage graduate and postdoctoral students, and especially those who aspire to careers as postsecondary faculty in SME&T disciplines, to become skilled teachers and current postsecondary faculty to acquire additional knowledge about how teaching methods affect student learning.

---

[25]The World Wide Web url is <http://www.wisc.edu/cels>

Graduate degree programs should provide graduate and postdoctoral students with training in the pedagogical skills they need to teach undergraduates effectively in classroom, laboratory, and field settings. In adopting **Vision 6**, universities also would provide all faculty with resources and opportunities for continuing professional development, informal education, and professional interaction with their higher education colleagues in order to help them enhance their professional skills and expertise as teacher-scholars throughout their academic careers.

Background

Recent reports on graduate education and postdoctoral experiences all point to a changing job market where alternatives to research careers in academe are becoming increasingly important for many Ph.D.s in a variety of fields (National Research Council, 1995b; Rice, 1996; Tobias et al., 1995; National Science Foundation, 1996a; Commission on Professionals in Science and Technology, 1997; Association of American Universities, 1998). It is emphasized that students who can work collaboratively, have high-level oral and written communication skills, and are expert in some aspect of SME&T but are also broadly trained are more employable than students who have taken a more narrow approach to their dissertations and career preparation.

Excellent teachers have all of these qualities, but too few SME&T graduate programs systematically encourage their development. In collaboration with the Council of Graduate Schools, some graduate schools recently have initiated comprehensive programs to introduce their students to the excitement and challenge of careers that emphasize teaching undergraduates or students in the nation's public schools.[26] However, it is more frequently the case that graduate programs in SME&T do not systematically prepare masters or Ph.D. candidates to work with undergraduates. Nor do these programs expose these advanced students to current issues in SME&T education that they will need to know for successful academic careers, especially at primarily teaching institutions that offer some of the best opportunities for employment. Indeed, graduate mentors

---

". . . we have not, as a nation, paid adequate attention to the function of the graduate schools in meeting the country's varied needs for scientists and engineers. There is no clear human-resources policy for advanced scientists and engineers, so their education is largely a byproduct of policies that support research. The simplifying assumption has apparently been that the primary mission of graduate programs is to produce the next generation of academic researchers. In view of the broad range of ways in which scientists and engineers contribute to national needs, it is time to review how they are educated to do so."

National Research Council, 1995b, pg. ES-3

"More than half of all doctoral students will seek employment in colleges and universities, 54 per cent according to the National Research Council's 1995 Survey of Earned Doctorates. The percentage of Ph.D.s who become faculty varies broadly between fields, ranging from 83 per cent of humanities majors to 22 per cent of engineering majors. Most future faculty, however, cannot realistically expect to find positions at the 3 per cent of the nation's colleges and universities that are research universities. Yet graduate education severely neglects the professional goal of the majority of students who will become college professors, that is to say, teaching."

Boyer Commission on Educating Undergraduates in the Research University, 1998, pgs. viii-1

---

[26]Additional information about this program is available at <http://www.cgsnet.org/programs/pff.htm>

may explicitly or implicitly discourage their students from spending too much time and effort preparing for careers in teaching if it "distracts" them from their research projects or lengthens the time needed for them to obtain their degree (Boyer Commission on Educating Undergraduates in the Research University, 1998).

Lack of preparation for teaching extends to the postdoctoral level. In some fields, Ph.D.s undertake two or more postdoctoral fellowships before finding more permanent positions (Commission on Professionals in Science and Technology, 1997; Association of American Universities, 1998, National Research Council, 1998c), yet few postdoctoral positions encourage or even permit opportunities to gain teaching experience.[27] This is true despite the aspiration of many postdoctoral fellows to careers in academe (Association of American Universities, 1998).

Lewis (1994) has argued that undergraduate education is the keystone for the education system in the United States because it prepares everyone who will go on to teach from kindergarten through the undergraduate years. Therefore, institutions of higher education not only have responsibility for preparing SME&T graduate and post-doctoral students for careers in research but also for preparing future teachers and providing current teachers with continuing education. In addition to acknowledging that they have all of these responsibilities, institutions of higher education should exercise these responsibilities with a high level of care, rigor, and

intellectual excitement. The importance of teaching and learning deserves no less.

Professionals in other fields are required to upgrade their skills continually and confront new issues in their disciplines (including teachers in grades K-12). Faculty who teach undergraduate and graduate students should have similar opportunities to upgrade and update their knowledge base and skills related to educational issues and pedagogy.

"Increasingly today's postdocs find themselves in 'no man's land.' Theirs is frequently an unstructured existence that is compounded by shortages in faculty positions, low salaries, little or no job security, and ever-tightening budgets. They are neither faculty members, with all the associated benefits and potential for tenure, nor are they student research assistants. In fact, some institutions have a dozen or more 'employment categories' for postdocs, so it is sometimes difficult to identify them. The long hours they log are juxtaposed against increasing lengths of time in postdocs, as they often opt to extend or start new ones. Their inability to secure permanent positions often is given as a reason for such extension of time as postdocs."

Commission on Professionals in Science and Technology, 1997, pg. 4

Strategies for Promoting and Implementing Vision 6

Executive and academic officers of postsecondary institutions can implement Vision 6 by

1. Working with graduate faculties to establish programs that integrate discussion of important current issues in teaching and learning while both faculty and graduate teaching assistants acquire new teaching skills.

   In 1997, Diamond and Gray (1998) conducted a survey of graduate students in a variety of disciplines (both inside and outside the natural sciences) at seven large public

---

[27]Some notable exceptions do exist. For example, the National Science Foundation sponsors a program of two-year Postdoctoral Fellowships in Science, Mathematics, Engineering, and Technology Education that provides up to 20 fellows per year with opportunities to develop ". . . the necessary skills to assume leadership roles in SME&T education in the nation's diverse educational institutions" and "expertise in a facet of science education research that would qualify them for a range of educational positions that will come with the 21st century." (NSF Bulletin 97-166.) NSF also sponsors the Integrative Graduate Education and Research Training (IGERT) program that emphasizes multidisciplinary projects (<http://www.ehr.nsf.gov/EHR/DGE/igert.htm>). In the private sector, the Camille and Henry Dreyfus Foundation offers senior faculty at predominately undergraduate institutions the opportunity to hire postdoctoral fellows. These fellows then have specific responsibilities to engage in teaching undergraduates.

and private research universities across the United States. These students were asked to indicate their major responsibilities as teaching assistants, the type and level of preparation they had received, and those aspects of teaching in which they wanted more preparation. When data from the 1997 survey were compared to data from a similar survey conducted at the same institutions 10 years earlier, Diamond and Gray found that greater numbers of graduate students were receiving more opportunities for training in teaching. The training identified included conducting classroom discussions, using audiovisual aids and instructional technology, and understanding university regulations about classroom and professional conduct.

"Because so much of teaching assistants' development takes place informally within departments, it is essential that structures be developed and maintained that encourage and support departmental faculty and administrators. Each new cohort of graduate students has the same needs and only through constant attention can the quality of their experience stay consistent over time. Improving that experience takes even greater effort, but such efforts [sic] can pay dividends on individual campuses and in individual departments in the preparation of future generations of faculty members."

Diamond and Gray, 1998, pgs. 18 and19

However, the survey also identified remaining trouble spots. For example, 25 percent of the 1997 survey respondents stated that they were being offered no formal preparation for their teaching responsibilities. Further, the surveys showed that the major responsibilities of teaching assistants had changed little: grading (97% of the respondents in both surveys) and conducting office hours for undergraduates (94% of respondents in both surveys). When the 1997 survey respondents were asked what additional

preparation they would like, they gave preference to self-evaluation, course evaluation, developments in technology, and classroom presentation. Three out of every four of the graduate student-respondents in the 1997 survey indicated that they planned to pursue academic careers.

Most likely, many of these students will find such positions in institutions other than research universities (Commission on Professionals in Science and Technology, 1997). Thus, graduate and postdoctoral programs should help prepare them for such employment by making available opportunities to study issues related to undergraduate teaching and to gain practical experiences as teaching assistants for undergraduate SME&T laboratories. These opportunities should be available as early in the graduate or postdoctoral careers of these students as possible.

Suggestions for developing effective programs for graduate students and examples of such programs in the biological sciences, chemistry, mathematics, and other disciplines can be found in Lambert and Tice (1993). Also, the Council of Graduate Schools, in collaboration with the American Association of Colleges and Universities, has established the "Preparing Future Faculty" program. This initiative encourages new approaches to graduate education for students in research institutions who are planning careers in academe by providing opportunities to practice teaching and to learn about the roles and responsibilities of faculty members at institutions that primarily serve undergraduates.[28]

2. Establishing arrangements with community colleges, other undergraduate institutions, and K-12 schools that allow graduate and postdoctoral students to experience teaching at these types of schools.

Opportunities for faculty positions at top-tier research institutions are diminishing

---

[28]Additional information about this program is available at <http://www.cgsnet.org/programs/pff.htm>

(National Research Council, 1995b, 1996e). Current data and projections indicate that two-year community colleges, K-12 schools, and four-year predominantly undergraduate institutions are where greater opportunities for employment will exist for a growing number of young scientists, mathematicians, and engineers in the United States. These changing demographics make it increasingly imperative for graduate and postdoctoral students in SME&T who wish to teach to have exposure to the lifestyles and responsibilities of faculty members in local community colleges, liberal arts colleges, and comprehensive universities (as encouraged by the Council of Graduate Schools; see also Strategy 1, page 55, and footnote 27), and to learn about the lifestyles and responsibilities of K-12 teachers. For example, more than 40 percent of the nation's undergraduates attend and may receive most of their postsecondary science and mathematics education from two-year institutions (National Science Foundation, 1997a), and that percentage is growing. Through the establishment of arrangements with local community colleges, graduate and postdoctoral students could gain invaluable teaching experience in lower-division courses and greater understanding of the needs of students who may not pursue additional education in SME&T. There also is a current and projected demand for K-12 teachers: at present, there is a shortfall in teachers certified in science and mathematics; and over the next decade, some two million K-12 teachers are expected to retire (Darling-Hammond, 1997).

3. Providing infrastructure that encourages graduate student and faculty access to publications, videos, and other materials that address the improvement of undergraduate teaching.

   Postsecondary institutions can make it easier for faculty and teaching assistants to examine these resources by purchasing enough copies for those who are interested. Copies of these materials should be made available at the campus Teaching and Learning Center (including through the Center's campus intranet or World Wide Web site or in the libraries of individual SME&T departments).

4. Encouraging appropriate academic departments and campus service units to assist graduates with preparing summaries of their work in a form accessible to the general public.

   Many graduate and postdoctoral students will elect careers that require them to employ public speaking and other oral and written communication skills. It is likely that, at some point, these students will need to explain their often highly technical work to audiences that lack the background to understand and appreciate that work. Graduate and postdoctoral training programs could begin to enhance students' abilities to address these and other audiences early in their careers. In addition to reporting on their work through the traditional venues—scholarly journals and presentations at professional meetings—graduate and postdoctoral students could be asked to prepare summaries or longer presentations of their work for inclusion in alumni magazines, departmental brochures and websites. These advanced students also could give talks at all-campus forums or local community organizations.

   Academic departments that might be engaged to teach graduate and postdoctoral students how to prepare clear, concise, and effective articles and presentations include offices of communications and departments in the SME&T disciplines themselves. Campus service units, such as the Office of Public Affairs, also could be involved. By using the work of students to announce new research results in the publications of an institution, both the institution and the students could benefit.

Individual faculty and academic departments can implement Vision 6 by

1. Encouraging departments to offer graduate and postdoctoral students opportunities to improve their teaching skills in laboratories, classrooms,

and in the field, even when such activities might compete with time dedicated to individual research.

Many graduate students work directly with SME&T undergraduates as teaching assistants in laboratories and discussion sections of courses, but they often have little opportunity to be involved with the many facets of preparing and teaching a whole course. Teaching assistantships should be designed to allow and encourage graduate and postdoctoral students to develop a broad array of effective inquiry-based teaching and learning skills in a variety of contexts. These acquired skills and experiences could instill in graduate and postdoctoral students a sense of the breadth of responsibilities that faculty assume as teachers, advisors, and mentors of undergraduate students in SME&T. Programs that have been recognized for their success in preparing the next generation of faculty are in place in a variety of institutions (e.g., examples in Lambert and Tice, 1993).

In addition, outside support from both federal agencies and private foundations is available. For example, the National Science Foundation administers the Postdoctoral Fellowships in Science, Mathematics, Engineering and Technology Education (<http://www.nsf.gov/cgi-bin/getpub?nsf 9917>). Examples from private foundations include the Cottrell Scholars Awards given by the Research Corporation to beginning faculty in chemistry and physics who excel at both research and teaching. (<http://www.rescorp.org>) and the Camille and Henry Dreyfus Foundation's teacher-scholar awards to strengthen teaching and research careers of faculty in the chemical sciences (<http://www.dreyfus.org/th.shtml#introduction>).

2. Serving as role models and mentors for graduate and postdoctoral students interested in pursuing careers in K-12 or postsecondary teaching.

Faculty can model effective teaching practices to graduate and postdoctoral students in many ways. In addition to providing these students with opportunities to observe and engage in teaching, faculty can convey the importance of the teaching enterprise by becoming intellectually engaged themselves in issues of teaching and pedagogy and by utilizing campus resources to improve their individual teaching skills. Faculty also can encourage their protégés to participate in workshops and seminars on teaching sponsored by professional societies. Faculty advisors can enhance the value of this exposure by accompanying their students to these sessions and by holding follow-up discussions with their research groups.

3. Asking invited speakers at departmental colloquia to discuss briefly aspects of their teaching as a routine part of the introduction to their scientific work or educational research.

Faculty mentors can indicate the importance of undergraduate teaching by describing their own teaching interests and accomplishments and inviting visiting speakers to do so as well. Presentations by speakers may emphasize their research interests and expertise, but, when appropriate, these speakers also could be asked to give a separate presentation about their teaching experiences or at least an opening statement about how the research to be described has been included in their teaching.

4. Reserving time at department meetings to discuss participation of graduate students in curriculum, assessment, and other educational issues.

Faculty whose departments encourage them to spend time discussing their work as teachers become more engaged in all aspects of providing quality undergraduate education (Kennedy, 1997). Both current and prospective faculty should engage as educators in intellectual discourse about teaching and learning that is similar to their engagement as researchers in discourse about research. Given that many graduate students and postdoctoral fellows highly value the securing of positions in academe, departments could invite colleagues from other types of postsecondary institutions to department meetings to discuss the requirements for and expectations of faculty members at those institutions. Graduate students and postdoctoral fellows might also be invited to provide peer assessments of faculty teaching.

5. As part of the interview process, asking faculty candidates to present a general lecture to undergraduates on a topic selected by the department or program or to give a pedagogical seminar to faculty and graduate students that discusses some aspect of teaching.

Expecting faculty candidates to present either a lecture to undergraduates on some aspect of the discipline or a seminar to faculty and graduate students in which the candidates discuss some aspect of teaching can send a powerful message to graduate students and prospective faculty members about the importance the department places on teaching.

See Appendix A for additional information about and strategies for implementation of **Vision 6** *as discussed during the Committee on Undergraduate Science Education's "Year of Dialogue" regional symposia and topical forums.*

CONCLUSION AND EPILOGUE

The visions articulated in this report are based on evidence provided by the scholarly literature and input from hundreds of people in the SME&T higher education community who spoke with the Committee on Undergraduate Science Education (CUSE) at its meetings or during the committee's regional symposia and topical forums. On this basis, these visions—and the accompanying implementation strategies—were designed to be applicable to many types of American post-secondary institutions. Some might claim that achieving meaningful reform across this range of institutions and on as broad a front as undergraduate SME&T education is nearly impossible, however. Indeed, when CUSE began work in 1993 to find ways to improve the scientific literacy of *all* undergraduates, many members wondered about the potential success of their mission. Subcommittees were formed to deal with curricular issues, teaching and learning issues, and the culture of higher education. Most members of the committee at that time was convinced that the third sub-committee faced the most difficult challenge. Changing any cultural paradigm that is deep-seated, that has served many of its members well, and that is at least tolerated by others *is* a difficult challenge, particularly when the desired change needs to be both substantial *and* sustainable.

Over the course of five years, CUSE discussed with hundreds of scientists, mathematicians, engineers, administrators, and others in both the higher education and pre-college SME&T communities how to produce *sustainable* change in SME&T education (e.g., see Preface and Appendix A). As a result of these discussions, the committee became firm in its resolve to focus on fundamental,

systemic reform of undergraduate SME&T education in the interests of advancing the levels of scientific literacy of all Americans. Committee members agreed with the prevailing view among representatives of higher education that fundamental changes in K-12 science and mathematics education are essential to any reform efforts. But they also took the view that improving undergraduate SME&T education is equally—and possibly even more—critical for achieving *lasting* improvement in SME&T education.

There have been so many attempts to introduce programs of large-scale reform to education, especially in the K-12 sector, that many faculty have adopted a "this, too, shall pass" attitude. CUSE members believe, however, that a variety of circumstances now conspire to induce long-lasting change in pre-college and postsecondary education in the United States. In addition to the findings and recommendations in this report, other recent reports from highly respected panels have emphasized the need for change in undergraduate SME&T education (e.g., National Research Council, 1996a; National Science Foundation, 1996b; Boyer Commission on Educating Undergraduates in the Research University, 1998; and "A Teachable Moment," a report from a Pew Science Program in Undergraduate Education roundtable discussion on the virtues of hands-on, inquiry-based approaches to science curricula and pedagogy [Institute for Research on Higher Education, 1998]). The recommendations in these reports about how to improve undergraduate education are quite similar. For example, the report from the Boyer Commission, the Pew roundtable, and this report all stress the importance of inquiry-based and interdisciplinary approaches to teaching and learning in the early undergraduate years and adequate preparation and experience in teaching for graduate students.

Other forces also are at work that postsecondary faculty, departments, and institutions increasingly must heed. National and statewide standards and curriculum frameworks are being implemented for K-12 science and mathematics education. Legislators in many states are demanding greater accountability and firm assurances from postsecondary faculty in public institutions that undergraduates are receiving a quality education (Boyer Commission on Educating Undergraduates in the Research University, 1998). Federal agencies, such as the National Science Foundation (1997b), increasingly are requiring proposals for research grants to indicate how the proposed research and its results will improve educational opportunities for students. Private foundations, such as the Howard Hughes Medical Institute, the Pew Charitable Trusts, and the Exxon Education Foundation, are now providing large-scale financial support to improve SME&T education at the K-12 and undergraduate levels.

The support for reform outside of postsecondary institutions is strong and compelling. Increasingly, the committee has witnessed support for changing SME&T education from inside these institutions, as well. This is heartening, for improvement in education can be truly successful only when those who must implement recommended reforms embrace them. In the five years of CUSE's existence, the members have seen evidence of increasing numbers of college and university SME&T faculty who recognize the need to restructure undergraduate SME&T education and who are willing to work individually and collaboratively toward that end. In addition, organizations that represent higher education and professional disciplinary societies are examining their roles in catalyzing educational change. Examples of programs sponsored by such organizations include

- Project Kaleidoscope's Faculty for the 21st Century (F21) program,[29] which is a five-year effort to locate and support up to 1,000 pre-tenured faculty in SME&T disciplines who have been recognized for their SME&T education potential. F21 members gather annually at national meetings to discuss and work through the many facets of changing undergraduate and K-12 education.

- New Experiences in Teaching (Project NExT)[30] and Workshop for New Physics Faculty,[31] which seek out newly appointed postsecondary faculty in mathematics and physics, respectively. These faculty then get together for several weeks during the summer to focus on quality teaching.

- The American Association for Higher Education's "Teaching Initiative," including the "Peer Review of Teaching Project,"[32] in which major universities have examined ways to incorporate peer review of teaching, especially formative review, into the evaluation of faculty performance.

- The National Research Council's newly initiated study of how the evaluation of SME&T teaching can be improved, which will consider the special circumstances involved with teaching in SME&T disciplines (e.g., teaching laboratories, field studies, and mentoring of undergraduate student researchers). This study also will examine how learning outcomes by students can be factored into teaching evaluations and how such approaches might provide a basis for ongoing professional development for SME&T faculty.

- The Council of Graduate Schools, which has sponsored the "Preparing Future

---

[29]Additional information about Faculty for the 21st Century is available at <http://www.pkal.org/faculty/f21/index.html>

[30]Additional information about Project NExT is available at <http://archives.math.utk.edu/projnext/>

[31]Additional information about the Workshop for New Physics Faculty is available at <http://www.aapt.org/programs/newnfc1.html>

[32]Additional information about this project is available at <http://www.aahe.org/>

Faculty" initiative[33] to enable graduate students at large research universities to experience first hand the roles and responsibilities of faculty members at a variety of institutions that serve undergraduate students.

- The presidents of postsecondary institutions affiliated with the Association of American Universities, who recently commissioned a "Task Force on K-16 Education" to explore how to define entrance requirements in light of K-12 reform standards, how to articulate introductory undergraduate course objectives, and how to prepare future teachers and provide continuing professional development to practicing teachers. (Recommendations were expected in 1998.)

- The increasing numbers of professional societies that are both recognizing members for effective teaching or public outreach in education and devoting time at their annual meetings to discussions of undergraduate SME&T education and to workshops to enable society members to share good ideas and practices in teaching and learning with colleagues. In December of 1997, representatives from a number of disciplinary societies convened at a conference on their role in improving SME&T education within their own disciplines and across disciplines. This activity was one of a series of symposia sponsored by the National Science Foundation (NSF) following the publication of its report, *Shaping the Future: New Expectations for Undergraduate Education in Science, Mathematics, Engineering, and Technology* (1996b). A summary report of the discussions held during this activity is available (Project Kaleidoscope, 1998). In addition, the Coalition for Education in the Life Sciences recently released a report on the role of professional societies in the life sciences in promoting education

(Coalition for Education in the Life Sciences, 1998).

- The actions of organizations with influence over specific disciplinary programs. For example, the Accrediting Board for Engineering and Technology (ABET) has introduced new and highly flexible program accreditation criteria that place more responsibility on postsecondary institutions to determine the mission and goals of their engineering programs. ABET also will expect these programs and their sponsoring institutions to demonstrate how the goals have been achieved. Engineering programs will be expected to demonstrate that their graduates have the fundamental knowledge and skills necessary to succeed in the engineering profession, including understanding the impact of engineering solutions to problems in global and societal contexts. In mathematics, the Joint Policy Board for Mathematics (JPBM), an organization that communicates the importance of mathematics to government officials and the public, recently established a task force "to provide the post-secondary mathematical community with resources for enhancing the educational activities of faculty." The task force is charged with helping "institutions and departments reflect on their educational missions, determine the range of educational activities that should 'count' in the promotion and tenure process given their missions, and document educational activities in reliable and meaningful ways."[34]

- Increasing numbers of reports and other publications, which provide specific examples and case studies of innovative undergraduate SME&T courses and programs (e.g., McNeal and D'Avanzo, 1997; Howard Hughes Medical Institute, 1996a).

- The Boyer Commission on Educating Undergraduates in the Research

---

[33]More information about this program is available at <http://www.cgsnet.org/programs/pff.htm>

[34]More information about this program is available at <http://www.maa.org/data/news/jpbm%2Deaf.html>

University's report (1998), which cites numerous examples of innovative undergraduate education programs at research universities.

- A recently released report, *The Integral Role of the Two-Year College in the Science and Mathematics Preparation of Prospective Teachers* (Virginia Collaborative for Excellence in the Preparation of Teachers, 1998), describes 11 exemplary science and math programs found in two-year colleges across the nation.

While these efforts are noteworthy and important, CUSE members believe that individual faculty, their departments, individual institutions of higher education, and umbrella organizations, such as professional disciplinary societies and higher education organizations, need to act together toward common goals. As suggested throughout this report, the undergraduate SME&T education enterprise involves too many players, objectives, and levels of engagement for change in any one component to have a significant, long-lasting impact by itself. As also indicated in this report, professional disciplinary societies and higher education organizations have particularly critical roles to play in bringing the component parts of the higher education system together. For example, these organizations can bring together innovators from different postsecondary institutions to share their successes and failures in improving SME&T education and to disseminate best practices beyond individual departments or institutions. In the end, dissemination of such information will have little effect unless individual faculty use that information to change their own teaching and to share their experiences with departmental and institutional colleagues.

Most faculty who would like to change their teaching in existing courses or, as recommended in this report (see **Vision 2** beginning on page 25) and elsewhere (e.g., Boyer Commission on Educating Undergraduates in the Research University, 1998), to create new courses that are truly interdisciplinary in scope and presentation, may not yet have the time, resources, or support and encouragement from their departments or institutions. CUSE members would urge faculty at least to try small, easily accomplished changes that could be evaluated for their efficacy and serve as the basis for additional improvements. For example, faculty could change an existing course in one way in each semester it is taught and base subsequent changes on feedback received from both current and former students and from colleagues.

Given their increasing emphasis on incorporating more real world examples and hands-on projects into courses and curricula and their traditional ties to industry, colleges of engineering can provide valuable insights and guidance to other science and mathematics departments that are looking to revamp their own programs. For these reasons, faculty and administrators in colleges of arts and sciences should consider consulting with their engineering colleagues for advice and feedback in this process. Faculty and administrators in other professional schools (e.g., schools of law and medicine) and at two-year colleges also might be in a position to provide examples of how courses have been revised to include more case studies and approaches to problem solving. All of these colleges and schools within postsecondary institutions have a vital interest in quality undergraduate SME&T programs. By working together, they can make changes to undergraduate SME&T courses and programs more dynamic and fruitful within their own programs as well as across the nation.

This type of recommendation also can be extended to SME&T departments. Change could begin by reserving one or two departmental meetings per semester to talk about the goals of the curriculum and what students emerging from courses in the department should know and be able to do after completing introductory and more advanced courses. Faculty who have revised their courses could discuss these changes with and solicit comments from departmental colleagues. SME&T departments also could invite colleagues from the school of education to one of those meetings (and vice versa!) to focus on issues of teacher preparation and professional development in science, mathematics, engineering, and technology. Graduate and postdoctoral students also could be invited. One or several presentations in the department's colloquium series during a semester or an academic year could be devoted to critical issues in SME&T teaching and learning.

What, ultimately, will change the predominant culture in institutions serving undergraduates? What will change the prevailing norms in undergraduate SME&T education and in the preparation of K-16 teachers of SME&T? We know much more now than we did even 10 years ago about how students learn (e.g., National Research Council, in press) and how to make good use of this knowledge in classrooms and laboratories (e.g., National Research Council, 1997a), **if we choose to do so**. Perhaps changes in practice will come from national and state efforts to provide standards for K-12 science and mathematics education that stand to give us greater confidence in coming years that more students who enter college are more well prepared in the SME&T disciplines than ever before. Perhaps it will be our willingness to capitalize on this better

preparation to provide undergraduate students with greater depth of understanding and appreciation of these subjects. Or to use information technology resources now available at previously unimaginable levels. Surely, change will occur when we take advantage of these resources—as individuals, departments, and institutions. Surely, it will occur when teaching and learning are viewed as worthwhile and important as other scholarly pursuits (Boyer, 1990).

The committee recognizes that implementing the visions of this report will require new funds or shifts in the allocation of existing resources from within postsecondary institutions. Depending on factors such as institutional governance and the progress that departments and institutions already have made in improving undergraduate SME&T education, costs may vary considerably from institution to institution. However, the evidence and information provided throughout the body of this report and the perspectives offered by participants at the regional symposia and topical forums (see Appendix A) suggest that change is both needed and, most likely, inevitable. The committee hopes that this report will stimulate serious discussions at all higher education institutions that also will take into account the need for new or reallocated resources to implement and support such change.

REFERENCES

Alberts, B. 1994. "What I learned from 30 years in the university about catalyzing change." In (Narum, J., [Ed.]) "What Works: Resources for Reform." *Occasional Paper II*. Washington, DC: Project Kaleidoscope.

American Association for the Advancement of Science. 1990. *The Liberal Art of Science: Agenda for Action*. Washington, DC: Author.

American Association for the Advancement of Science. 1993. *Benchmarks for Science Literacy*. New York: Oxford University Press.

American Association for the Advancement of Science. 1997. *Resources for Science Literacy*. New York: Oxford University Press.

American Chemical Society. 1990. *Innovative Approaches to the Teaching of Introductory Chemistry*. Washington, DC: Author.

American Chemical Society. 1997. "Chemistry in the *National Science Education Standards:* A Reader and Resource Manual for High School Teachers." Washington, DC: Author.

Anderson, E., (Ed.). 1993. *Campus Use of the Teaching Portfolio: Twenty-five Profiles*. Washington, DC: American Association for Higher Education.

Arons, A.B. 1990. *A Guide to Introductory Physics Teaching*. New York: John Wiley and Sons.

Association of American Universities. 1998. "Committee on Postdoctoral Education: Report and Recommendations." Washington, DC: Association of American Universities. Also available at <http://www.Tulane.edu/~aau/PostdocEducationReport.html>

Atkin, J.M., and Atkin, A. 1989. *Improving Science Education Through Local Alliances*. Santa Cruz, CA: Network Publications.

Baker, W., and Gifford, B. 1997. "Technology in the classroom: from theory to practice." *Educom Review* 32(5): Also available at <http://www.educom.edu/ web/pubs/ pubHomeFrame.html>

Bell, J.A., and Buccino, A. (Eds.). 1997. "Seizing Opportunities: Collaborating for Excellence in Teacher Preparation." Washington, DC: American Association for the Advancement of Science.

Benjamin, R., and Carroll, S. 1993. "Restructuring higher education—by design." *Rand Institute on Education & Training, Issue 2*. San Jose, CA: Rand Institute.

Benson, S.A., and Yuan, R.T. 1998. "The university classroom as a virtual workplace." In (Selden, S. [Ed.]) *Essays in Quality Learning: Teachers' Reflections on Classroom Practice*. Pgs. 73-81. College Park, MD: University of Maryland Press.

Biological Sciences Curriculum Study. 1993. *Developing Biological Literacy: A Guide to Developing Secondary and Post-secondary Biology Curricula*. Colorado Springs, CO: BSCS Innovative Science Education.

Boyer, E.L. 1990. *Scholarship Reconsidered: Priorities of the Professoriate*. Princeton, NJ: Carnegie Foundation for the Advancement of Teaching.

Boyer Commission on Educating Undergraduates in the Research University. 1998. *Reinventing Undergraduate Education: A Blueprint for America's Research Universities*. Menlo Park, CA: Carnegie Foundation for the Advancement of Teaching. Also available at <http://notes.cc. sunysb.edu/ Pres/boyer.nsf>

Bybee, R.W. 1998. "Improving precollege science education—the involvement of scientists and engineers." *J. Coll. Sci. Teaching* 27(5):324-328.

Centra, J., Froh, R.C., Gray, P.J., and Lambert, R.M. 1987. *A Guide to Evaluating Teaching for Promotion and Tenure*. Littleton, MA: Copley Publishing Group.

Cheney, L.V. 1989. "Foundations of the Natural Sciences: 8 hours." From "50 Hours: A Core Curriculum for College Students." Washington, DC: National Endowment for the Humanities.

Clinton, W.J. , and Gore, A. 1994. "Science in the National Interest." Washington, DC: Office of Science and Technology Policy.

Coalition for Education in the Life Sciences. 1992. "Report of the National Life Science Education Conference II." Racine, WI: Wingspread Conference Center.

Coalition for Education in the Life Sciences. 1998. "Professional Societies and the Faculty Scholar: Promoting Scholarship and Learning in the Life Sciences." Madison, WI: Coalition for Education in the Life Sciences.

Commission on Professionals in Science and Technology. 1997. "Postdocs and Career Prospects: A Status Report." Washington, DC: Commission on Professionals in Science and Technology.

Council of Chief State School Officers. 1997. "Mathematics and Science Content Standards and Curriculum Frameworks: States Progress on Development and Implementation, 1997." Washington, DC: Author. Also available at <http://www. ccsso.org/pdfs/framework.pdf>

Darling-Hammond, L. (Ed.). 1997. "Doing What Matters Most: Investing in Quality Teaching." New York: National Commission on Teaching and America's Future.

Devlin, K. 1998. "Rather than scientific literacy, colleges should teach scientific awareness." *Chronicle of Higher Education* 64(20):B6.

Diamond, R.M., and Adam, B.E. (Eds.). 1993. *Recognizing Faculty Work: Reward Systems for the Year 2000. New Directions for Higher Education* (No. 81). San Francisco: Jossey-Bass Publishers.

Diamond, R.M., and Gray, P.J. 1998. "1997 National Study of Teaching Assistants." Syracuse, NY: Syracuse University Center for Instructional Development.

Diez, M.E., Richardson, V., and Pearson, P.D. 1993. *Setting Standards and Educating Teachers: A National Conversation.* Washington, DC: American Association of Colleges for Teacher Education.

Edgerton, R., Hutchings, P., and Quinlan, K. 1991. T*he Teaching Portfolio: Capturing the Scholarship in Teaching.* Washington, DC: American Association for Higher Education.

Education Trust. 1998. "Education Watch: The 1998 Education Trust State and National Data Book, Vol. II." Washington, DC: Education Trust.

Ehrmann, S.C. 1995. "The bad option and the good option." *Educom Review,* 30 (5). Also available at <http://www.educom. edu/web/pubs/pubHomeFrame.html>

England, J., Hutchings, P., and McKeachie, W.J. 1996. "The professional evaluation of teaching." *ACLS Occasional Paper* No. 33. New York: American Council of Learned Societies.

Fox, M.A. 1998. "Improving undergraduate science education: national initiatives, local implications." *J. Coll. Sci. Teaching* 27:373-375.

Gabel, D.L. (Ed.). 1994. *Handbook of Research on Science Teaching and Learning.* New York: Macmillan Publishing Co.

Glassick, C.E., Huber, M.T., and Maeroff, G.I. 1997. *Scholarship Assessed: Evaluation of the Professoriate.* San Francisco: Jossey-Bass.

Gray, P.J., Diamond, R.M., and Adam, B.E. 1996. *A National Study on the Relative Importance of Research and Undergraduate Teaching at Colleges and Universities.* Syracuse, NY: Center for Instructional Development, Syracuse University.

Hawkins, E.F., Stancavage, F.B., and Dossey, J.A. 1998. "School Policies and Practices Affecting Instruction in Mathematics: Findings from the National Assessment of Educational Progress." (NCES 98-495) Washington, DC: National Center for Education Statistics. Also available at <http://www.nces.ed.gov/ pubsearch/pubsinfo.asp?pubid=98495>

Hazen, R.M., and Trefil, J. 1991. *Science Matters: Achieving Scientific Literacy.* New York: Doubleday.

Howard Hughes Medical Institute. 1995. "Science Education: Expanding the Role of Science Departments." Report of the Undergraduate Program Directors Meeting, October 3-5, 1994. Chevy Chase, MD: Howard Hughes Medical Institute.

Howard Hughes Medical Institute. 1996a. *Beyond BIO 101.* Chevy Chase, MD: Howard Hughes Medical Institute.

Howard Hughes Medical Institute. 1996b. "1997 Undergraduate Program Directory: Grants Awarded to Colleges and Universities 1992-1996." Chevy Chase, MD: Howard Hughes Medical Institute.

Hurd, P.D. 1994. "Technology and the advancement of knowledge in the sciences." *Bull. Sci. Tech. Soc.* 14(3):125-131.

Hutchings, P. 1993. *Using Cases to Improve College Teaching.* Washington, DC: American Association for Higher Education.

Hutchings, P. 1996. *Making teaching community property: a menu for peer collaboration and review.* Washington, DC: American Association for Higher Education.

Institute for Research on Higher Education. 1998. "A teachable moment." *Policy Perspectives* 8 (1): 1-10.

Ireton, M.F.W., Manduca, C.A., and Mogk, D.W. (Eds.). 1996. *Shaping the Future of Undergraduate Earth Science Education: Innovation and Change Using an Earth System Approach.* Washington, DC: American Geophysical Union.

Joint Policy Board for Mathematics. 1994. "Recognition and Rewards in the Mathematical Sciences." Washington, DC: American Mathematical Society. Also see http://www.maa.org/data/news/jpbm%2Deaf. html>

Jones, R.C. 1994. "First-year science students: their only year?" *J. Coll. Sci. Teaching* 23(6):356-362.

Juillerat, F., Dubowsky, N., Ridenour, N.V., McIntosh, W.J., and Caprio, M.W. 1997. "Advanced placement science courses: high school—college articulation issues." *J. Coll. Sci. Teaching* 27:48-52.

Kennedy, D. 1997. *Academic Duty.* Cambridge, MA: Harvard University Press.

Kirwan, W.E. 1994. "Reform and national standards: implications for the undergraduate education and professional development of science and mathematics teachers." *Sigma Xi, Scientists, Educators, and National Standards: Action at the Local Level.* (Forum Proceedings) pgs. 51-63. Research Triangle Park, NC: Sigma Xi, the Scientific Research Society.

Lambert, L.M., and Tice, S.L. (Eds.). 1993. "Preparing Graduate Students to Teach: A Guide to Programs that Improve Undergraduate Education and Develop Tomorrow's Faculty." Washington, DC: American Association for Higher Education.

Langenberg, D.N. 1997. "Reforming both houses: schools and higher education." *Thinking K-16* 3(1):1-2. Washington, DC: The Education Trust.

Leitzel, J.R.C. (Ed.). 1991. "A Call for Change: Recommendations for the Mathematical Preparation of Teachers of Mathematics." Washington, DC: Mathematical Association of America.

Lewis, S.R. 1994. "Some economics of effective science education." (Narum, J.[Ed.]) "What works: resources for reform." *Occasional Paper II.* Washington, DC. Project Kaleidoscope.

Lowery, L. (Ed.). 1997. "NSTA Pathways to the Science Standards: Elementary School Edition." Arlington, VA: National Science Teachers Association.

Massy, W.F., Wilger, A.K., and Colbeck, C. 1994. "Overcoming 'hollowed' collegiality." *Change* 26(4): 10-20.

Mazur, E. 1997. "Peer Instruction: A User's Manual." Upper Saddle River, NJ: Prentice Hall.

McDermott, L. 1990. "A perspective on teacher preparation in physics and other sciences: The need for special science courses for teachers." *Am. J. Phys.* 58(8):734-742.

McNeal, A.P., and D'Avanzo, C.D. (Eds.). 1997. *Student Active Science: Models of Innovation in College Science Teaching.* Fort Worth, TX: Harcourt Brace & Company.

Moore, J.A. 1993. *Science as a Way of Knowing: The Foundations of Modern Biology.* Cambridge, MA: Harvard University Press.

Moore, J.A. 1995. "Cultural and scientific literacy." *Molec. Biol. Cell* 6:1-6.

Narum, J. (Ed.). 1995. "Structures for Science: A Handbook on Planning Facilities for Undergraduate Natural Science Communities." Washington, DC: Project Kaleidoscope.

National Academy of Sciences. 1997. "Preparing for the 21st Century: The Education Imperative." Washington, DC. National Academy Press.

National Academy of Sciences. 1998. *Teaching About Evolution and the Nature of Science.* Washington, DC: National Academy Press.

National Commission on Excellence in Education. 1983. "A Nation at Risk: The Imperative for Educational Reform." Washington, DC: U.S. Government Printing Office.

National Commission on Teaching and America's Future. 1996. "What Matters Most: Teaching for America's Future." New York: National Commission on Teaching and America's Future.

National Council of Teachers of Mathematics. 1989. *Curriculum and Evaluation Standards for School Mathematics.* Reston, VA: Author.

National Council of Teachers of Mathematics. 1991. *Professional Standards for Teaching Mathematics.* Reston, VA: Author.

National Education Goals Panel. 1997. "The National Education Goals Report: Mathematics and Science Achievement in the 21st Century." Summary. Washington, DC: Author.

National Research Council. 1982. *Science for Non-Specialists: The College Years.* Washington, DC: National Academy Press.

National Research Council. 1989. "Everybody Counts: A Report to the Nation on the Future of Mathematics Education." Washington, DC: National Academy Press.

National Research Council. 1990. *Fulfilling the Promise: Biology Education in the Nation's Schools.* Washington, DC: National Academy Press.

National Research Council. 1991. *Moving Beyond Myths: Revitalizing Undergraduate Mathematics.* Washington, DC: National Academy Press.

National Research Council. 1995a. *Engineering Education: Designing an Adaptive System.* Washington, DC: National Academy Press.

National Research Council. 1995b. *Reshaping the Graduate Education of Scientists and Engineers.* Washington, DC: National Academy Press.

National Research Council. 1996a. *From Analysis to Action: Undergraduate Education in Science, Mathematics, Engineering, and Technology.* Report of a Convocation. Washington, DC: National Academy Press.

National Research Council. 1996b. *National Science Education Standards*. Washington, DC: National Academy Press.

National Research Council. 1996c. *The Preparation of Teachers of Mathematics: Considerations and Challenges*. Washington, DC: National Academy Press.

National Research Council. 1996d. *The Role of Scientists in the Professional Development of Science Teachers*. Washington, DC: National Academy Press.

National Research Council. 1996e. *Careers in Science and Engineering*. Washington, DC: National Academy Press

National Research Council. 1997a. *Science Teaching Reconsidered: A Handbook*. Washington, DC: National Academy Press.

National Research Council. 1997b. *Science Teacher Preparation in an Era of Standards-Based Reform*. Washington, DC: National Academy Press.

National Research Council. 1997c. "Introducing the National Science Education Standards." Washington, DC: National Academy of Sciences.

National Research Council. 1997d. "Improving Teacher Preparation and Credentialing Consistent with the *National Science Education Standards:* Report of a Symposium." Washington, DC: National Academy Press.

National Research Council. 1997e. "Preparing for the 21st Century: The Education Imperative." Washington, DC: National Academy Press.

National Research Council. 1998a. "Developing a Digital National Library for Undergraduate Science, Mathematics, Engineering, and Technology Education: Report of a National Research Council Workshop." Washington, DC: National Academy Press.

National Research Council. 1998b. "Every Child A Scientist: Achieving Scientific Literacy for All (How to Use the *National Science Education Standards* to Improve Your Child's School Science Program.)" Washington, DC: National Academy Press.

National Research Council. 1998c. "Trends in the Early Careers of Life Scientists." Washington, DC: National Academy Press.

National Research Council. In press. *"How People Learn: Brain, Mind, Experience, and School."* Washington, DC: National Academy Press.

National Science Foundation. 1992. "America's Academic Future: A Report of the Presidential Young Investigator Colloquium on U.S. Engineering, Mathematics, and Science Education for the Year 2010 and Beyond." Washington, DC: National Science Foundation.

National Science Foundation. 1993. "Proceedings of the National Science Foundation workshop on the role of faculty from the scientific disciplines in the undergraduate education of future science and mathematics teachers." (NSF 93-108) Washington, DC: National Science Foundation.

National Science Foundation. 1996a. "Indicators of Science and Mathematics Education, 1995."Arlington, VA: National Science Foundation. .

National Science Foundation. 1996b. *Shaping the Future: New Expectations for Undergraduate Education in Science, Mathematics, Engineering, and Technology*. (NSF 96-139) Arlington, VA: National Science Foundation.

National Science Foundation. 1997a. "National Science Foundation Activities in Support of Two-Year College Science, Mathematics, Engineering, and Technology Education: A Report of the Division of Undergraduate Education. Fiscal Year 1996 Annual Report." (NSF 97-165) Arlington, VA: National Science Foundation.

National Science Foundation. 1997b. "Grant Proposal Guide. " (NSF 98-2) Arlington, VA: National Science Foundation.

National Science Foundation. 1998a. "Undergraduate Education: Science, Mathematics, Engineering, Technology. Program Announcement and Guidelines." (NSF 98-45) Arlington, VA: National Science Foundation.

National Science Foundation. 1998b. "Information Technology: Its Impact on Undergraduate Education in Science, Mathematics, Engineering, and Technology. Report of an NSF Workshop." (NSF 98-82) Arlington, VA: National Science Foundation.

National Science Foundation. 1998c. "Teacher Preparation and NSF Collaboratives for Excellence in Teacher Preparation: FY97 Awards." (NSF 98-99) Arlington, VA: National Science Foundation.

National Science Resources Center. 1998. *Resources for Teaching Middle School Science*. Washington, DC: National Academy Press.

Oblinger, D.G. 1995. "Total Quality Management in Higher Education: A Continuous Improvement Process." *International Business Machines Report Series*. Also available at <http://ike.engr. washington.edu/news/whitep/tqm.html>

Office of the President, University of California. 1991. "Report of the University-wide Task Force on Faculty Rewards." Oakland, CA: Office of the President, University of California.

Oregon University System. 1998. "Proficiency Standards: Summary Charts of Criteria for All Content Areas." Eugene, OR: Proficiency-based Admissions Standards System, Oregon University System. Also available at <http://pass-ous. uoregon.edu>

Ostwald, T. 1994. "Successful collaborations between scientists and schools." *Sigma Xi, Scientists, Educators, and National Standards: Action at the Local Level.* (Forum Proceedings) Pps. 179-181. Research Triangle Park, NC: Sigma Xi, the Scientific Research Society.

O'Sullivan, C.Y., Weiss, A.R., and Askew, J.M. 1998. "Students Learning Science: A Report on Policies and Practices in U.S. Schools." (NCES 98-493) Washington, DC: National Center for Education Statistics. Also available at <http://nces.ed.gov/pubsearch/pubsinfo.asp?pubid=98493>

Pister, K.S., and Rowe, M.B. 1993. "The Federal Investment in Science, Mathematics, Engineering, and Technology Education: Where Now? What Next? Report of the Expert Panel for the Review of Federal Education Programs in Science, Mathematics, Engineering, and Technology." Washington, DC: Federal Coordinating Council for Science, Engineering and Technology.

President and Fellows of Harvard University. 1993. "Choosing Courses to Prepare for College." Cambridge: Harvard University Press.

Project Kaleidoscope. 1991. *What Works. Building Natural Science Communities: A Plan for Strengthening Undergraduate Science and Mathematics, Vol. I.* Washington, DC: Project Kaleidoscope.

Project Kaleidoscope. 1994. *What Works. Leadership: Challenges for the Future. Vol. II.* Washington, DC: Project Kaleidoscope.

Project Kaleidoscope. 1997. "The Question of Reform: Report on Project Kaleidoscope 1996-1997." Washington, DC: Project Kaleidoscope.

Project Kaleidoscope. 1998. *Shaping the Future of Undergraduate Science, Mathematics, Engineering and Technology Education: Proceedings and Recommendations from the PKAL Day of Dialogue.* Washington, DC: Project Kaleidoscope.

Ramo, S. 1988. *The Business of Science: Winning and Losing in the High Tech Age.* New York: Hill and Wang.

Redish, E., and Rigden, J. (Eds.). 1997. "The Changing Role of Physics Departments in Modern Universities." *AIP Conference Proceedings.* 399.

Reese, C.M., Miller, K.F., Mazzeo, J., and Dossey, J.A. 1997. "National Assessment of Educational Progress 1996 Mathematics Report Card for the Nation and the States." Washington, DC: National Center for Education Statistics.

Rice, R.E. 1996. "Making a place for the new American scholar." Inquiry #1. *Working Paper Series on New Pathways: Faculty Careers and Employment for the 21st Century.* Washington, DC: American Association for Higher Education.

Riley, R.W. 1998. "An end to 'Quiet Backwaters': universities must make teacher education a much higher day-to-day priority." Speech given at the National Press Club. Reprinted in *Chronicle of Higher Education* 45(6):B10.

Rotberg, Iris C. 1998. "Interpretation of International Test Score Comparisons." *Science* 280: 1030-1031.

Rutherford, F.J., and Ahlgren, A. 1990. *Science for All Americans.* New York: Oxford University Press.

Schmidt, W.H., and McKnight, C.C. 1998. "What can we really learn from TIMSS?" *Science* 282:1830-1831.

Seldin, P. 1998. "How colleges evaluate teaching: 1988 vs. 1998." *AAHE Bulletin* 50(7):3-7.

Seymour, E., and Hewitt, N.M. 1997. *Talking about Leaving: Why Undergraduates Leave the Sciences.* Boulder, CO: Westview Press.

Shulman, L.S. 1993. "Teaching as community property: putting an end to pedagogical solitude." *Change* 25:6-7.

Stalheim-Smith, A., and Scharmann, L.C. 1994. "General biology: creating a positive learning environment for elementary education majors." *Amer. Biol. Teacher* 56:216-220.

Texley, J., and Wild, A. (Eds.). 1996. "NSTA Pathways to the Science Standards: High School Edition." Arlington, VA: National Science Teachers Association.

Thorsen, C. 1994. "Strategies for building university partnerships." *Sigma Xi, Scientists, Educators, and National Standards: Action at the Local Level.* (Forum Proceedings) Pgs. 143-147. Research Triangle Park, NC: Sigma Xi, the Scientific Research Society.

Tobias, S. 1990. *They're Not Dumb, They're Different: Stalking the Second Tier.* Tucson, AZ: Research Corporation.

Tobias, S. 1992. *Revitalizing Undergraduate Science: Why Some Things Work and Most Don't.* Tucson, AZ: Research Corporation.

Tobias, S., Chubin, D.E., and Aylesworth, K. 1995. *Rethinking Science as a Career: Perceptions and Realities in the Physical Sciences.* Tucson, AZ: Research Corporation.

University of Wisconsin System. 1997. "University of Wisconsin Competency-Based Admission: Admission Competencies, Rating Scale, and Standardized Reporting Profile." (Provisional Document) Madison, WI: University of Wisconsin System.

Uno, G. 1997. *Handbook on Teaching Undergraduate Science Courses: A Survival Training Manual.* Norman, OK: University of Oklahoma Printing Services.

U.S. Department of Education. 1997. "Postsecondary Persistence and Attainment" in "The Condition of Education 1997." Washington, DC: U.S. Government Printing Office.

U.S. Department of Education. 1998a. "Third International Mathematics and Science Study." Washington, DC: National Center for Education Statistics.

U.S. Department of Education. 1998b. "Promising Practices: New Ways to Improve Teacher Quality." Washington, DC: U.S. Government Printing Office. Also available at <http://www.ed.gov/ pubs/PromPractice/>

van der Vink, G.E. 1997. "Scientifically illiterate vs. politically clueless." *Science* 276:1175.

Virginia Collaborative for Excellence in the Preparation of Teachers. 1998. "The integral role of the two-year college in the science and mathematics preparation of prospective teachers." *Journal of Mathematics and Science: Collaborative Explorations* 1(2):1-135.

Watson, R.F. 1998. "The need for more school-teachers in science and math: How colleges can help." *Chronicle of Higher Education* 45(6):B9-10.

Wergin, J. 1994. "The Collaborative Department: How Five Campuses Are Inching Toward Cultures of Collective Responsibility." Washington, DC: American Association for Higher Education.

Williams, W., and Ceci, S.J. 1997. " 'How'm I doing?': problems with student ratings of instructors and courses." *Change* 29(5):13-23.

Wilson, J.M. (Ed.). 1996. *Proceedings of the Conference on the Introductory Physics Course: On the Occasion of the Retirement of Robert Resnick.* New York: John Wiley and Sons, Inc.

Wulf, William A. 1998. "Education for an Age of Technology." June 26. Washington, DC: National Academy Op-Ed Service.

Yates, A. 1995. "Higher education has a link to real reform at the K-12 level." *The Denver Post.* April 29:8b.

APPENDIX A

OVERVIEW OF THE COMMITTEE ON UNDERGRADUATE SCIENCE EDUCATION'S REGIONAL SYMPOSIA AND TOPICAL FORUMS

Regional Symposium Series and Topical Forums: Introduction

On April 9-11, 1995, the National Research Council (NRC) and the National Science Foundation (NSF) jointly hosted a national convocation, "From Analysis to Action: Undergraduate Education in Science, Mathematics, Engineering, and Technology," at the National Academy of Sciences in Washington, DC. Over the next 18 months, the NRC's Committee on Undergraduate Science Education (CUSE) capitalized on the intellectual energy generated by that convocation and report (*From Analysis to Action*, National Research Council, 1996a) and by the subsequent release by NSF of *Shaping the Future* (National Science Foundation, 1996b) by sponsoring four one-day regional symposia and 10 one-day topical forums. These meetings were designed to advance and extend to a larger audience the national discussion about improving undergraduate science, mathematics, engineering, and technology (SME&T) education. With financial support from the Exxon Education Foundation, the committee worked with universities, scientific associations, and corporations to ensure that the symposia and topical forums were attended by a broad cross section of constituents vested in the issues under discussion.

CUSE's goals for the meetings were to articulate new ideas for improving undergraduate SME&T education and to expand on strategies that encourage implementation of the recommendations contained in the NRC and NSF reports. Members of CUSE did not expect the one-day meetings to lead to major breakthroughs in addressing the challenge of increasing science literacy. Rather, the symposia and topical forums were designed to elicit information and perspectives from a wider spectrum of the SME&T higher education community than had participated in the April 1995 convocation in Washington. The meetings also were intended to catalyze and encourage ongoing dialogue among educators, administrators, and higher education policy makers about the need for greater scientific literacy in American undergraduate students.

The symposia and topical forums were very effective in drawing attention to a set of issues that rarely had received sufficient attention during previous meetings attended by a wide range of stakeholders in higher education. During the CUSE-sponsored events, participants expressed their appreciation for the opportunity to interact with colleagues from local, regional, and state postsecondary institutions with highly variable educational missions. They were eager to share their concerns and challenges about undergraduate SME&T education and to report on and discuss informally promising courses and programs.

The discussion of issues and the sharing of information during these events helped CUSE formulate the vision statements that form the body of this report. Therefore, references are made here to specific sections of the report, and, likewise, references are made in the main report to the roles and contributions of the regional symposia and topical forums.

Summarized below are the structure, demographics, main themes, and topics of the symposia, first, then of the topical forums. Both the regional symposiums and the topical forums were exceedingly important in helping the members of CUSE to identify and analyze the most important issues that must be confronted by those who wish to improve undergraduate SME&T education. The wealth of ideas that emerged from the hundreds of participants served as the basis for the vision statements and strategies for implementation that are included in this report. Participants' commitment to sustainable improvement of undergraduate SME&T education surely will be critical to the success of subsequent efforts.

Regional Symposium Series: Structure and Demographics

The four symposia were held in different regions of the United States and hosted by a variety of institutions, organizations, and agencies from the academic, business, and government sectors. The dates, locations, and hosts of the symposia are listed in Table 1.

Invitations and announcements for the four symposia were disseminated to attract participation from a broader spectrum of stakeholders in the SME&T education community than could be present at the national convocation held in Washington in April of 1995.

Before each symposium, registrants received copies of the reports, *From Analysis to Action* and *Shaping the Future* to provide a common context for discussions at the symposia. Registrants also were polled about the recommendations in *From Analysis to Action*. The recommendations of most interest to registrants for any given symposium were then highlighted for discussion, and registrants were so notified. The committee also asked registrants to share information or visions for overcoming obstacles to implementing the recommendations in the report. The agendas for each symposium also included other issues identified by the registrants as critical for improving undergraduate science education.

Attendance at each symposium ranged from 101 to 145 participants. Registrants included SME&T faculty, postsecondary institution administrators, K-12 teachers, business leaders, representatives from federal and state education agencies, and executives and program officers from public and private foundations. Appendix B lists the institutional affiliations of participants (pg. 88).

Regional Symposia: General Themes

The national convocation in Washington featured an "Options for Action" structure that allowed participants to discuss and recommend to the convocation organizers various strategies for overcoming barriers to improving undergraduate SME&T education. The committee adopted a similar structure for the regional symposia, with discussions

TABLE 1 DATES, LOCATIONS, AND HOSTS OF THE FOUR REGIONAL SYMPOSIA

Date	Location	Host
October 16, 1995	Ann Arbor, Michigan	University of Michigan
November 10, 1995	Waltham, Massachusetts	GTE Laboratories
January 19, 1996	Houston, Texas	Johnson Space Center, National Aeronautics and Space Administration
February 1, 1996	Claremont, California	Pomona College

focused around three themes: "Options for Action for Students," "Options for Action for Faculty," and "Options for Action for Institutions." Symposia discussions of these themes are synthesized and summarized below. Topics that received the most attention tended to be national in scope. Topics emphasized at a particular regional meeting are delineated as such. Discussion points are summarized to convey the breadth of issues covered at the meetings.

At all of the regional symposia, participants raised many common issues regarding the current state of science education in the United States. They included issues that have been noted in previous reports on education, beginning with *A Nation at Risk* (National Commission on Excellence in Education, 1983). These served as gambits for the general discussion that followed about how to improve undergraduate SME&T education. Once participants had raised several initial sub themes and issues, they proceeded to discuss solutions as well as obstacles likely to be encountered. Main topics that were raised repeatedly appear in boldfaced type.

Theme I: Options for Action for Students

Registrants often began discussions under this theme by commenting that the mediocre science and mathematics preparation of many incoming college students may be impeding their readiness to pursue SME&T courses as undergraduates. Participants also felt that students seem reluctant to tackle challenging SME&T subjects in college. Attendees remarked on the general lack of motivation and diligence among students, including students in upper-division courses who are SME&T majors.

At each symposium, some participants speculated on whether appropriate **pre-college preparation for SME&T education** could be prescribed (see text related to **Vision 1**). There was discussion about faculty establishing informal guidelines in collaboration with college admissions offices that would indicate the level of mathematical and scientific knowledge and skills that entering students would need to go on successfully to complete lower-division undergraduate SME&T courses. The mention of guidelines led to discussions of the impact of national and state K-12 mathematics and science education standards and curriculum frameworks now—and in the future—on the background and interest levels of incoming SME&T students. Participants at the symposium in Houston were particularly concerned about how the pre-college preparation of students might affect the postsecondary community (see also "Theme II: Options for Action for Faculty" below for further discussion of K-12 standards).

Participants in all of the regional symposia seemed to agree that the level of preparation in SME&T for most incoming college students is inadequate, and they raised the issue of what the postsecondary system could or should do to assuage the problem. Participants asked how enterprising universities should be in attracting to the natural sciences students whose incoming skill levels are weak.

In discussing the level of preparation of today's students to undertake college-level work in SME&T, participants seemed particularly concerned with recurring evidence of the lack of access and exposure to high-quality pre-college SME&T education for some students, particularly those from groups historically underrepresented in these disciplines. Discussions of how to address this issue tended to differ by region. Participants' concepts of and ideas about **equity, access,** and **exposure** also emerged. Some of the participants pointed to the need for each postsecondary institution to develop a coherent, focused plan to improve SME&T education that includes informal linkages with K-12 education. Such partnerships would forge a more cohesive and synchronous SME&T educational continuum for grades K-16. At the symposium in Claremont, participants whose institutions have been affected by judicially or legislatively mandated dismantling of affirmative action programs indicated a high level of concern about the potential impact of these actions on K-12 education and students' access to college. Participants commented that it would be helpful if entities such as the NRC or the NSF could identify programs that successfully motivate and support women and minorities to move through the science and engineering "pipelines" at the undergraduate and graduate levels.

Another topic discussed at all the symposia was high school **Advanced Placement (AP)** courses in science and mathematics (see additional text on this topic in **Vision 1**, beginning on page 22). Some participants questioned whether AP courses are beneficial for students. They observed that by allowing students to be exempted from college-level courses, AP courses in mathematics and science may interfere with the goal of producing more scientifically literate students. Simply stated, students who receive high scores on AP exams and place out of college graduation requirements in mathematics or science as undergraduates will not benefit from innovative efforts to improve technological and scientific literacy among college students.

When asked to compare the quality of introductory undergraduate SME&T courses with AP courses, many participants in all of the symposia expressed cautious satisfaction with the organization and structure of post-secondary courses for declared SME&T majors. However, some participants noted studies showing some student dissatisfaction with these courses (e.g., Seymour and Hewitt, 1997), and it was suggested that administrators, faculty, and other interested constituents review how they could be better organized and presented.

This suggestion typically led to a discussion of **requirements for SME&T majors** (see additional discussion of this topic in the report, beginning on page 26). Participants remarked that it might be counterproductive to isolate students majoring in SME&T from creative reform efforts aimed at non-majors.

Some participants suggested that reforms being instituted in introductory SME&T courses for non-majors would likely offer valuable insights into how to revamp upper-level SME&T courses for majors.

Participants expressed great interest in **infusing genuine inquiry-based undergraduate research opportunities** into the science curriculum, particularly in introductory courses. Many participants stated that it is problematic to provide hands-on opportunities that mirror genuine scientific experiences only to students who reach upper-division courses because "late bloomers" in SME&T could become discouraged while waiting for such opportunities. Also at risk are students who demonstrate an initial enthusiasm for science but then lose it while taking the typical undergraduate progression of courses. Participants did mention constraints imposed by accreditation boards and disciplinary societies as a barrier to innovation in courses for majors. Also discussed was the importance of including representatives from accreditation boards in departmental and other meetings when reform measures are discussed.

In discussing **requirements for non-science majors**, many participants agreed that the lower-division undergraduate curriculum for non-science majors needs reshaping and revitalizing. They also recognized that a major barrier to this revitalization is ambiguity about what non-science majors should know, understand, and appreciate about SME&T. Which content is essential? What attitudes and perceptions are particularly harmful or useful? Participants wondered whether teaching style needed to be considered when developing appropriate content. Attendees recognized that these questions interfaced with the issue of standards for post-secondary SME&T education. Because universities and colleges have diverse missions and the overwhelming majority of faculty highly value this institutional heterogeneity, standards-setting across the postsecondary environment was seen as too challenging, too threatening, and, ultimately, too unprofitable to be pursued.

Some participants questioned whether it was in anyone's best interest to isolate or segregate majors from non-majors in lower-division courses. This discussion complemented comments about the preparation of students for interdisciplinary or science teaching careers at the pre-college level and how this preparation would benefit from dismantling the separation of courses for SME&T majors and non-majors. Many participants in the symposium at Waltham thought that **interdisciplinary undergraduate courses** offered great promise either to invigorate (in the case of incoming students) or to reinvigorate (in the case of students already enrolled) interest in SME&T. However, some participants at this regional symposium were especially concerned about the many obstacles to creating such courses.

In addition to the issue of interdisciplinary course work, some participants were keenly interested in the preparation of students for careers in SME&T, including as **future pre-college teachers** (see additional discussion of this topic in the section on **Vision 4** in the report). One question was, what can universities do to convince faculty in undergraduate science departments to bring their courses more in synchrony with the national K-12 mathematics and science standards and to model teaching styles that would be effective for standards-based teaching at the pre-college level. Participants also wondered how discipline-based professors could be encouraged to recognize their tremendous influence on future teachers to the degree that they would then become more inclined to incorporate important aspects of the mathematics and science standards into their curriculum and classroom practice.

Finally, many participants expressed a strong frustration with what could be characterized as **societal issues and challenges**— issues such as students' inability to think or reason independently or to maintain motivation and interest in subject matter. While concrete suggestions for combating these types of barriers were not offered, some participants

conjectured that standards-based reform could have a positive impact. Discovery-oriented learning environments and technology-based instruction might positively influence this area as well. All participants expressed hope that multimedia instruction might assist in increasing or at least maintaining student interest and motivation in SME&T.

Depending on their perspective, many participants were upbeat about the new skills the mathematics and science standards could help students acquire. In particular, many expected the standards to ensure competence in mathematics and reading comprehension (assuming that the standards backlash is neutralized), and stated that this would overcome many of the problems with incoming students identified in the opening discussions.

Theme II: Options for Action for Faculty

Faculty issues elicited a less vigorous discussion at these four symposia than issues perceived to be student-related (see "Theme I: Options for Action for Students"). A major faculty issue that arose dealt with balancing teaching and research and how these two aspects of a faculty member's responsibilities could be better integrated. Participants were keenly aware that the **pedagogy** employed in classrooms should be informed by educational research just as is the content covered in SME&T disciplines. It was recognized, however, that faculty are encumbered by many demands and that undertaking pedagogical studies or attending to pedagogical research literature are frequently postponed activities.

Participants considered ways to make effective **hands-on laboratory experiences** available in lower-division courses without significantly increasing the number of personnel required to do so. There was particular interest in fostering an environment that encouraged faculty to create curricula using multiple media and to experiment with new technologies for more effective teaching. Throughout the symposium series, many attendees saw **information technology** as a liberating tool for many faculty and one that presaged more creativity in the structuring and delivery of SME&T courses. Beyond their general enthusiasm for increased use of information technology in postsecondary SME&T curriculum, participants recognized that what constitutes effective use has not yet been well defined. A final concern expressed was how to expand cooperative learning skills in the undergraduate science and engineering classes.

Participants also broached the subject of **preparation and development of SME&T professionals** (see discussion of these topics in the **Vision 6** section of the report). Discussions centered on preparing doctoral candidates for leadership roles at community colleges or in teaching lower-division SME&T courses for non-majors. Participants noted that tackling the challenges of supply and demand for Ph.D. positions is problematic, as well as investigating alternative, creative career paths available to SME&T majors outside of academia (see also National Research Council, 1995b).

Symposia participants also raised, but did not discuss at length, another issue of concern to many of them—how to assess and evaluate accurately and fairly the teaching performance of faculty.[35]

Theme III: Options for Action for Institutions

Participants acknowledged and confirmed that chancellors, presidents, provosts, and other high-level administrators representing the interests of their institutions are essential partners in implementing any plans to improve the science literacy of the general postsecondary student population. Attendees agreed that some issues related to modernizing the teaching of SME&T disciplines must

be under the purview of administrators, including **recognition and reward structure**. The need to change the traditional faculty reward structure so that it encourages faculty to manage their teaching duties more responsibly and effectively was a commonly heard refrain. Many participants agreed that executive and academic officers of postsecondary institutions must decide on a plan of action to align recognition and rewards with a more equitable set of expectations for research, teaching, and service. They observed that, in a balanced reward structure, research contributions would not compensate for teaching inadequacy. The majority of attendees felt that, at the very least, institutional administrators must champion the implicit obligation of faculty to teach undergraduate SME&T students well.

As described in the previous section ("Theme II: Options for Action for Faculty"), participants proposed implementation of more hands-on activities in lower-division SME&T courses but also felt that administrative involvement was important. Several participants strongly encouraged administrators to make available the resources needed to allow faculty to provide more inquiry-based laboratory experiences to all students. Participants stated that the excitement of offering such an approach for more introductory students might, in turn, inspire increased faculty enthusiasm. Greater student engagement and greater student competence in SME&T might be the ultimate rewards.

Another proposal for administrators that also received general support throughout the symposium series centered on postsecondary institutions engaging in **K-12 and industry partnerships**. It was suggested that administrators could play a greater role in motivating and rewarding individual faculty and program units to establish partnerships with K-12 schools or industry. The goals would include

- helping K-12 schools locally and regionally to align with national and their state's standards for mathematics and science;

---

[35]The NRC's Committee on Undergraduate Science Education will oversee a project to examine special circumstances related to the evaluation of teaching by SME&T faculty and how such evaluations might be tied to student learning outcomes and continuing professional development. Additional information about this project will be available in late 1998 from the NAS Main Web Page under "Current Projects," as well as from the Center for Science, Mathematics, and Engineering Education's home page, <www2.nas.edu/center/>

- championing the effective incorporation of information technology into the K-12 SME&T curriculum;

- strengthening the access of all pre-college students, including minorities and women, to K-12 SME&T courses;

- seeking out and initiating partnerships, summer internships, or activities beyond the school environment to update the skills and knowledge of pre-college teachers in the SME&T disciplines.

Attendees speculated about industry's opinion of the content of undergraduate SME&T courses and the knowledge and skills that industry expects or would like graduates to possess. A small number of business and industry representatives attended the symposia, so these questions were not answered definitively. However, some representatives suggested that, where feasible, postsecondary institutions involve industry in education discussions.

Finally, many participants acknowledged that **funding issues** in relation to education reform (see discussion of **Vision 5** in the report) are a perpetual challenge for institutional administrators. Nonetheless, many participants felt it was extremely important for executives within postsecondary institutions to examine and implement many of the suggestions raised during the symposium series for improving undergraduate SME&T education. Participants urged administrators to accept assistance and guidance from faculty in what they projected to be a long and time-consuming process.

Regional Symposium Series: Conclusion

As revealed in the summaries given above, the symposium series was very useful in catalyzing broad conversations among a diverse set of education representatives interested in improving K-12 and undergraduate SME&T education. Attendees at all four symposia touched on many of the daunting challenges postsecondary institutions face in the current era of reform. These include educating all students to become more scientifically literate, incorporating valuable and realistic scientific experiences into undergraduate SME&T courses, and balancing rewards and recognition for faculty among their primary responsibilities of research, teaching, and community service. Participants in all four of the symposia showed keen interest in having postsecondary institutions clearly and forcefully articulate renewed commitment to teaching and a judicious appreciation for innovation and research by faculty who are trying to become better teachers.

Finally, participants stated their strong appreciation for networking opportunities offered by meetings such as the regional symposium series. Participants noted that such meetings encourage interactions between constituents from diverse educational communities and perspectives, permitting discovery of common concerns, solutions, achievements, and the sharing of information, experiences, and findings. Institutions such as the NRC and sponsors such as the NSF and Exxon Education Foundation were urged to continue hosting meetings such as these symposia to continue regional dialogues about improving SME&T education.

Topical Forums: Overview

The 10 one-day topical forums were held after the four regional symposia. CUSE designed the forums to explore more specific issues in undergraduate SME&T education with a variety of scientific and educational audiences. The symposium series was an opportunity for a broader constituency to initiate discussions on issues associated with making scientific literacy a priority for all undergraduates. Host organizations for the forums assisted CUSE in identifying topics for discussion and in formulating agendas. CUSE members helped focus the topical forums to give participants opportunities to devise practical solutions to overcome those barriers identified or discussed in the regional symposia. Where possible, CUSE revisited the issues raised in the symposia series to gain as broad a perspective as possible for articulating the visions and strategies for implementation found in this report.

Topical Forums: Structure and Demographics

The 10 topical forums were conducted between October 10, 1996 and May 1, 1997. Forum dates, topics, hosting organizations, locations, and number of participants are given in Table 2. For nine of the forums, participants were asked to pre-register, although some people attended who had not. The forum held at the annual meeting of the American Society of Limnology and Oceanography was announced in the meeting program, and participants were not asked to pre-register. Attendance at the topical forums was more variable than at the regional symposia (see Table 2 for attendance figures).

Many of the forums were held in conjunction with annual or regional meetings of professional associations and societies, as professional development activities on university campuses, or, in one instance, via a multi-site video conference link as a cooperative activity with the Florida State Department of Education. Because of the diverse agendas for the different forums, attendance ranged from 15 to 125 participants, and the length of time for these sessions ranged from one hour to a full day. Wherever possible and appropriate, invitations were extended to people outside the hosting organization, such as local K-12 teachers, business leaders, federal and state education representatives, and foundation executives. The partnerships formed between CUSE and the organizations that hosted each of topical forums gave committee members additional opportunities to engage postsecondary educators and administrators in discussions about changes needed in postsecondary education and factors that may be impeding such changes. Indeed, by scheduling

some of these forums in conjunction with other types of activities, such as annual meetings, CUSE was able to engage people from the SME&T community who were unable—or otherwise might not have elected—to participate in the regional symposia.

Topical Forums: Synopses

A synopsis of each forum is presented below, grouped into one of three categories: forums hosted by 1) Professional Organizations and Associations, 2) Universities, and 3) a State Educational Organization. Each synopsis contains cross-references to the specific visions contained in the body of this report.

Forums Hosted by Professional Organizations and Associations

National Council of Teachers of Mathematics (NCTM): This half-day forum was held in conjunction with a regional meeting of the NCTM. It focused on communication between SME&T faculty and faculty in schools of education in **creating and fostering effective interdisciplinary courses** that complement educational goals articulated in K-12 mathematics and science standards (see additional discussion in the section on **Vision 2** in the report). As a result of similar discussions at the regional symposium hosted by GTE, this topical forum highlighted effective interdisciplinary programs and collaborations among faculty in different kinds of postsecondary institutions.[36] The forum also gave participants the time and opportunity to consider the characteristics of a successful interdisciplinary program. The intention was to encourage forum participants to replicate similar courses at their own institutions.

Forum participants—both SME&T and education faculty—acknowledged that interdisciplinary courses can be very challenging

---

[36]Courses highlighted at this forum have been taught at the University of Missouri, Columbia, Kansas State University, and the University of Missouri, St. Louis.

TABLE 2 DATES, TOPICS, HOSTING ORGANIZATIONS, LOCATIONS, AND NUMBER OF PARTICIPANTS OF THE TEN TOPICAL FORUMS

Date	Forum Topic	Host	Location and Number of Participants
October 10, 1996	Productive Partnerships: Collaborations between Science, Mathematics, and Education Faculty for the Improvement of Teacher Education	National Council of Teachers of Mathematics Regional Meeting	Kansas City, MO 13 participants
October 15, 1996	Involving Research Faculty in the Reform of Undergraduate Science Education	University of Texas at Austin	Austin, TX 53 participants
November 8, 1996	Minority Access and Recruitment in the Sciences	City University of New York, Medgar Evers College	Brooklyn, NY 60 participants
November 14, 1996	Implications of Standards-based Education for Introductory College Science Courses	Florida Department of Education	Tampa, FL (7 sites) 269 participants total
November 18, 1996	Developing Scientific Literacy through Environmental Science Courses and Programs	Society for Environmental Toxicology and Chemistry	Washington, DC 16 participants
December 14, 1996	Addressing the Needs of the Workplace in Earth Science Classes	American Geophysical Union	San Francisco, CA 24 participants
December 28, 1996	Implications of the *National Science Education Standards* for Teacher Preparation	National Science Teachers Association's "Global Summit on Science and Science Education"	San Francisco, CA 30 participants
February 9, 1997	Limnology and Oceanography: Meeting the Needs of Non-Science Majors in Introductory Courses	American Society of Limnology and Oceanography	Santa Fe, NM 21 participants
January 28, 1997	Strategies for Developing Interdisciplinary Courses for Non-Science Majors	University of Washington System	Seattle, WA 87 participants
May 1, 1997	Integration of Pedagogy and Content Courses for Future Teachers	Center for Education and Equity in Mathematics, Science, and Technology, California State Polytechnic Institute	Pomona, CA 35 participants

to organize, implement, and maintain. After examining the characteristics of successful interdisciplinary programs, forum participants engaged in an active investigation of the steps required to produce similar programs to meet the needs of a wider range of students, including science majors and K-12 teaching majors.

Featured at this forum were comprehensive, introductory courses designed to bridge the natural sciences and humanities. They reflected, in part, national standards in mathematics and science. Participants in the forum were urged to view such courses as an effective way to impress upon students—especially prospective K-12 teachers—the importance and significance of SME&T in their lives (a perspective that would later be reflected in **Vision 2** of this report).

Society for Environmental Toxicology and Chemistry: This forum was held in conjunction with the annual meeting of this society, and several CUSE members attended to conduct a half-day break-out session. Entitled "Developing Scientific Literacy through Environmental Science Courses and Programs," the session provided an opportunity for members of CUSE to interact with environmental scientists on ways to **enhance the general scientific literacy** of environmental science students (see this discussion of **Vision 2** in this report). Participants reviewed environmental science programs from different postsecondary institutions, including several being taught at the University of Oklahoma, as follows: "Interdisciplinary Perspectives on the Environment" (Department of Philosophy), "Environmental Policy and Administration" (Energy Center), "Environmental Evaluation and Management" (School of Civil Engineering and Environmental Science), "The Ecology of the Greco-Roman Mediterranean" (Department of Classics), and "Principles of Plant Ecology" (Department of Botany). Another course, "Environmental Science," offered at Trinity College in Washington, DC, also was examined. Participants then discussed the creation of

additional programs for non-science majors that would link environmental concepts in interesting, informative, and creative ways.

American Geophysical Union: This half-day forum was conducted as a workshop that used earth science and geological exploration as the basis for discussion. Participants identified various skills that their students are expected to master in undergraduate courses and that might be needed in the modern work environment. Conversation centered mainly on skills for science majors, although participants noted that students with other interests and career aspirations also need many of these skills. The skills identified included

- *Ability to undertake scientific inquiry*
  - Define a scientific question
  - Plan a way to answer the question scientifically
  - Use scientific equipment
  - Analyze data
  - Interpret results

- *Ability to create products of scientific inquiry—data*
  - Maintain an organized and detailed laboratory notebook
  - Develop data sets
  - Produce diagrams that allow students to relate variables to one another

- *Ability to communicate the product of the scientific inquiry—oral reports*
  - Organize presentations for coherence and conciseness
  - Effectively present data and conclusions
  - Prepare visual aids
  - Syntax and grammar

- *Ability to communicate the product of the scientific inquiry—written reports*
  - Organize presentations for coherence and conciseness
  - Effectively present data and conclusions

- Interpret data
- Prepare written reports of high quality, using proper English
- Prepare illustrations

By using such criteria, participants felt that faculty could structure classroom assignments to provide students with the skills they must learn to become educated people and to satisfy SME&T employers.

The practical discussion that took place during the workshop presaged **Vision 2** of this report—making science an integral and integrated part of students' college experience.

National Science Teachers Association (NSTA): This forum was held in conjunction with NSTA's "Global Summit on Science and Science Education." Participants collectively reflected on the **changing emphases in content, teaching, assessment, and professional development** that can be expected as the *National Science Education Standards* and the National Council of Teachers of Mathematics (NCTM) *Curriculum and Evaluation Standards for School Mathematics* are adopted and implemented. Many of the suggestions and comments that arose during this forum mirrored those from the symposium series and influenced almost all of the vision statements and rationales offered in the body of this report.

Many participants in this forum recognized the importance of **teaching science content courses well.** By entrusting introductory and gateway courses to faculty members with exceptional teaching ability, colleges and universities can help ensure that all students are exposed to important concepts as well as to the processes of SME&T that are critical to enhancing scientific literacy and lifelong learning. A corollary raised by participants was that colleges and universities also must encourage and support faculty in their own pursuit of lifelong learning and scholarship.

Another important issue raised at this forum involves the role and responsibility of SME&T faculty at all types of institutions to **prepare prospective K-12 teachers of science and mathematics.** Because this is such

a vital but often overlooked role of faculty in SME&T disciplines and because the mathematics and science standards encourage an inquiry-based style of teaching, future teacher candidates should be encouraged to teach science to younger children. They could do so by engaging in innovative practicum experiences and other activities as part of their own pre-service educational experience. Furthermore, once new teachers have acquired basic skills and knowledge in these approaches to teaching, they—as well as more experienced teachers—must be afforded additional, extensive in-service training within school districts throughout their professional careers. Participants at this forum recommended that classes where future teachers practice their teaching be small enough to encourage innovation, creativity, and risk-taking. However, some participants cautioned that new and additional assessment tools are still needed to gauge learning that is consistent with the goals and approaches of the current K-12 science and mathematics education standards. (See additional discussion of these topics in the section on **Vision 5** in the report.)

Participants at this forum also discussed the level of preparation expected of entering students (reflected in **Vision 1**), providing innovative interdisciplinary courses that spark students' interest in a variety of educational pathways (reflected in **Vision 2**), and systematic evaluation of courses (reflected in **Vision 3**). Participants also mentioned the need to change incentives and rewards for innovative teaching (reflected in **Vision 5**) that would, in part, lead to improved programs for preparing prospective K-12 teachers of mathematics and science (reflected in **Vision 4**).

American Society of Limnology and Oceanography: This topical forum took place in conjunction with the society's annual meeting. The conversation at this forum focused on **how to tailor introductory courses to enhance the scientific literacy of students.** Participants agreed that a primary goal of *all* SME&T courses should be to teach students about the scientific method. Forum participants agreed that understanding this fundamental way of thinking about science would enhance students' general scientific literacy and their ability to understand specific scientific issues more clearly. Attendees also agreed that hands-on experiences generated via field trips are effective in realizing this goal. Participants suggested that by using familiar societal concerns (e.g., an environmental issue on or near the campus) as starting points, science courses, particularly those for non-science majors, could be enhanced. Such concerns could then lead to exploration of which scientific principles are needed to understand and address the issues.

Forum participants also indicated that central repositories of information, such as **web sites** that provide useful **information for non-science majors in introductory courses**, could also be very useful to faculty members who are interested in revamping and revitalizing their courses. Useful resources that could be disseminated in this fashion include laboratory exercises, video clips, case studies, other useful web pages, examples of "bad science," and information about how scientific understanding about some issue or problem develops and evolves.[37]

Attendees called for the **realignment of faculty rewards and recognition** at postsecondary institutions to recognize those faculty who have redesigned their courses in innovative ways, especially those courses aimed at non-science majors. Finally, forum registrants encouraged postsecondary institutions to make **graduate teaching assistantships** more prestigious. The value and relevance of teaching assistantships to graduate students would be emphasized by collaborative workshops for scientists, teaching assistants, and K-12 teachers and broad distribution of resources on effective teaching strategies. Professional societies also could influence the

national undergraduate SME&T reform effort and add to the prestige and distinction of teaching by sponsoring educational sessions at regional and national conferences, collaborating with other professional societies (Project Kaleidoscope, 1998), and seeking new and innovative ways to encourage teaching excellence at the postsecondary level.

Forums Hosted by Universities

University of Texas at Austin: During this half-day seminar, faculty were encouraged to recognize their **obligations and contributions to teaching**. Forum leaders noted that high-quality, innovative approaches to teaching can inspire SME&T majors and other students alike to appreciate and value these subjects. As one participant observed, "Individuals can appreciate science without being a scientist, just as individuals can appreciate art or music without being an artist or musician. However, both scientists and non-scientists need a cultural basis for understanding theory and scientific phenomena."

Included in this general discussion of improving SME&T courses for both majors and non-majors was a call for SME&T faculty to present their courses as they practice their professions.

Because research universities wield such great influence over the **rewards and recognition** structures typically found in the postsecondary community, participants in this forum pointed out that research universities also could have a great deal of influence over the improvement of teaching in their own institutions and elsewhere. Participants agreed that faculty and administrators in research universities carry an enormous responsibility because they either can perpetuate or change the current balance of rewards and recognition for teaching, research, and service. Participants concluded that creating a more scientifically literate citizenry is such a worthy goal that faculty must acknowledge the pivotal role of introductory SME&T courses in preparing students for technologically

---

[37]The National Science Foundation is beginning to address the need for such a resource. See footnote on page 36 of this report for additional information.

challenging careers and commit to improving them for all of their lower-division undergraduate students.

Acknowledging that such changes will require shifts in the culture of research universities, participants in this forum offered several straightforward suggestions, including the following:

- Researchers should highlight their teaching during guest lectures or when speaking at their own or other institutions.

- Researchers should ask guest speakers and lecturers at professional conferences and other academic events to convey information about their teaching.

- At least one departmental research seminar in a colloquium series could be devoted to a discussion of educational issues and pedagogy. Such a meeting also could be constructed to inform faculty of the most current research on science teaching, as well as K-12 education reform efforts.

- SME&T faculty could engage in greater collaboration with colleagues in their institution's school of education. A good beginning would be inviting education faculty to meetings of SME&T departments to inform SME&T faculty about best teaching practices.

- Because research SME&T faculty have the best perspectives of the "cutting edge of knowledge" in their disciplines, they could collaborate with education faculty who are knowledgeable about pedagogy and methodology. Together, these faculty could design exciting and modern courses and programs.

To enhance their ability to teach diverse student populations, faculty at research universities could collaborate with their colleagues at two-year colleges, who generally have developed greater expertise in this area. Such collaboration also would benefit faculty at two-year colleges by increasing their exposure to cutting edge research that could be incorporated into their courses.

Discussion at this University of Texas forum also centered around two other positive outcomes of excellent teaching: the expectation of increased scientific literacy among all students and the creation of the next generation of K-12 teachers. The forum informed many of the vision statements in this report, predominantly **Visions 4**, **5**, and **6**. In addition, discussion at this forum about the role of university faculty in preparing prospective K-12 teachers to teach SME&T in a style commensurate with national mathematics and science standards is reflected in **Vision 1**.

Medgar Evers College (City University of New York): The theme for this day-long workshop aimed at community college personnel was how to weave SME&T into the required undergraduate curriculum so that all students could become more scientifically literate. Participants discussed several critical barriers that discourage and often prevent **minority and other underrepresented students** from pursuing SME&T courses. Strategies to remove those barriers also were discussed.

Participants at this forum believed that introductory SME&T courses should be both gateways to careers in SME&T and to general literacy in these subjects. Attendees recognized that two-year colleges could and should play an important role in attracting students from diverse backgrounds to higher education. Indeed, as the demographics of the United States continue to change over the next century, some participants suggested that the expertise two-year colleges have in meeting the needs of a diverse student population would be instructive to four-year colleges and universities. For example, low-income students often need to work to support themselves through college or have familial obligations that impinge on study time but should not be permitted to thwart their educational goals. Furthermore, these students often cannot afford to take more than the minimum number of science courses unless they expect to major in a SME&T discipline. Therefore, the SME&T courses that they do take should be rigorous, emphasize the interrelationships among disciplines, incorporate information technology effectively, and include an inquiry-based laboratory experience. This expectation would enable students to become scientifically literate and to pursue a B.S. or beyond at four-year colleges or universities. In addition, prospective teachers, many of whom begin and sometimes complete their SME&T requirements at two-year colleges, would be better prepared to conduct standards-based teaching at the K-12 level. Participants emphasized that, to meet these goals, increased dialogue and collaboration between all the higher education institutions is important and, indeed, necessary.

An enduring challenge for postsecondary faculty, and especially those at two-year colleges, is addressing shortcomings in the educational backgrounds of entering students. This problem can have an impact on advising, career focus and aspirations, and retention of students. Participants agreed strongly that postsecondary institutions must, as central priorities, commit both to recruiting and admitting motivated students *and* to instituting programs that improve the likelihood of retaining those students throughout their undergraduate careers. Colleges and universities should admit capable students and then nurture them toward graduation and fulfillment of their professional and personal goals. In addition, they stated that university faculty cannot simply dismiss the present weaknesses of the pre-college educational system. Rather, faculty must consider methods to impart remedial and college-level information and skills quickly and engagingly so that students remain enrolled in SME&T courses and perhaps even elect to major in a SME&T discipline. Participants agreed that introductory courses could be constructed to fill gaps in knowledge and understanding that students bring to college from the high schools. Participants also suggested that partnerships be built between high schools, two-year colleges, four-year colleges, community-based organizations, and industry to make education a seamless process. One participant reported that, at

Medgar Evers College (a four-year campus of CUNY that offers both associate and baccalaureate degrees), the restructuring of calculus, physics, and chemistry courses into a workshop format has helped retain minority students. In addition, once students have completed the course, they then serve as workshop leaders for other students. Also, an on-campus learning center provides tutoring, collaboration, and information about career opportunities and presentation skills, as well as acts as a home base for students who need supplemental instruction. Medgar Evers faculty and administrators see the learning center not as a remediation resource but as providing an alternative method of teaching and learning that has benefited their students.

Students at two-year colleges who seek careers in teaching, especially those who will teach in the primary grades, may take all of their required courses in science and mathematics before transferring to a four-year institution. Therefore, the quality and diversity of SME&T courses at two-year colleges strongly influences what knowledge and skills they take to teaching but also whether students decide to continue to take SME&T courses at a four-year institution and thus become eligible for secondary teaching certification. For both primary and secondary grade teachers, two-year colleges play a critical role in teacher preparation.[38] In light of this, it was suggested that prospective teachers at two-year institutions could become involved in peer communities, where they could discuss issues related to teaching and provide encouragement to one other. Another suggestion was that students could become involved in professional activities to more closely link them to faculty mentors and help them build bridges between the academic and professional communities. Finally, participants noted that students need assistance in securing positions that can provide both meaningful work and income.

---

[38]Also see reference in this report to the Virginia Collaborative for Excellence in the Preparation of Teachers article on the role of two-year colleges in the preparation of future K-12 teachers of mathematics and science.

University of Washington System (UW): This forum, held at UW in Seattle, focused on identifying strategies to create **interdisciplinary courses within the SME&T disciplines**. A panel briefly discussed issues and opportunities in developing interdisciplinary courses, then participants divided into four break out groups to discuss strategies for developing different kinds of interdisciplinary courses that would launch students towards greater scientific literacy and lifelong learning. Attendees also considered possible institutional impediments to the development of such courses. The four areas considered by these break out groups were capstone courses, courses for non-majors, courses for future K-12 teachers, and courses for undergraduates completing general education requirements in SME&T. The plenary was then reconvened to share ideas and conclusions from the break out sessions.

Common issues that have an impact on the creation of interdisciplinary courses were identified by all four break out groups. For example, how to allocate credit to participating departments was identified as a barrier to the creation of interdisciplinary courses. Because students are required to take certain courses, they may be precluded from taking interdisciplinary courses. Students and their advisors also might perceive interdisciplinary courses to be more demanding or, conversely, less rigorous than required courses in traditional subject areas. To overcome these problems, attendees recommended that advocates of interdisciplinary courses strive for buy-in from academic advisors, all the science departments, registrars, and perhaps even from the institution's office of student affairs. Most participants agreed that another important variable in creating successful interdisciplinary courses is the personal compatibility of faculty members who work together in the effort. Building camaraderie, particularly when courses involve faculty from different departments, takes time but is nonetheless vital to forging a coherent, focused interdisciplinary course or program that can synthesize and achieve multiple academic goals.

Discussion from this forum informed the creation of **Visions 2, 3**, and **5** of this report.

California State Polytechnic University (CSPU): Participants at this topical forum sponsored by CSPU's Center for Education and Equity in Mathematics, Science, and Technology in Pomona considered 1) ways to develop working relationships between SME&T and education faculty in the preparation of teachers and 2) effective collaborations among SME&T faculty, education faculty, and K-12 schools.

To promote effective collaboration among such a diverse set of faculty stakeholders, participants urged universities to provide more recognition and rewards to faculty who focus on improving education. Attendees also suggested that postsecondary institutions could enhance teaching and learning in both SME&T departments and schools of education by offering joint appointments for qualified faculty so that they would have credibility and influence in both the SME&T and education communities. Others suggested that real improvement will require a "triad" approach that encourages student teachers, master teachers, and community college and university faculty to work together on projects that would improve teacher preparation and professional development.

Introductory courses were again identified at this forum as a pivotal point of influence in a student's academic career. To enhance student interest in and understanding of SME&T, attendees believed that introductory courses should be restructured to include a balanced perspective of history, philosophy, ethics, and applications in relation to SME&T disciplines. Some participants also suggested the development of new integrated science majors by rearranging existing courses rather than developing new ones. CSPU offers such an integrated program for certification of SME&T.[39]

---

[39]More information about CSPU's integrated programs is available at <http://www.intranet.csupomona.edu/~sci/descript.html>

This forum's final theme was the state of pre-college science and mathematics education. Many participants urged the postsecondary community to lend active support to K-12 education reform by adjusting college admission requirements and SME&T courses to reflect the current national standards for K-12 mathematics and science. In addition, participants said that courses for prospective teachers should not simply mimic courses for science majors but should be more specifically attuned to teachers' needs. Some participants wondered whether there should be special content courses for future teachers and, if so, how to decide what those courses should contain. However, most participants agreed that prospective teachers should learn their science as other science students do. Thus, their **science methods courses should be taught in science buildings and should include laboratories.** Courses should be taught in ways that students will be expected to teach in their own classrooms. Early field placement was also considered an essential component of effective preparation of K-12 teachers so that these students can apply as soon as possible the information, skills, and techniques they learn in their college classrooms and laboratories.

Discussions from this forum helped the committee prepare **Visions 2, 4, and 5.**

Forum Hosted by a State Educational Organization

Florida Department of Education: This forum, although physically based in Tampa, was an interactive teleconference with participants at seven sites around the state. It examined the implications of standards-based education for introductory college science courses.

Participants began by considering the opportunities and challenges that **national and state mathematics and science education standards** might present to undergraduate SME&T education. For example, as K-12 mathematics and science reform efforts become more ingrained in the K-12 system,

students from different schools systems might increasingly be expected to matriculate at post-secondary institutions with a greater parity of skills and understanding in SME&T. If these students come to their college study of SME&T with greater experience in inquiry-based and collaborative learning, they may have different expectations for their postsecondary learning experiences. Therefore, university administrations and faculty should consider how they will respond to new expectations.

One way that postsecondary institutions might prepare is by creating cross-disciplinary task forces that could spearhead new programs for prospective SME&T teachers and other SME&T-based disciplines. For example, teachers of both science and mathematics should learn how to help their students develop quantitative reasoning skills. More coherent integration of pedagogy and SME&T content in undergraduate courses that have been aligned with the goals and objectives of the science and mathematics standards could facilitate this goal. A more systemic plan could involve developing and implementing a capstone course for prospective teachers that integrates SME&T content and methods and is in concert with the goals and expectations of the NRC's *National Science Education Standards* and the National Council of Teachers of Mathematics standards for curriculum and professional development. Practicing teachers could collaborate with college faculty in the development of such courses to enhance course effectiveness and simultaneously to gain valuable professional development.

As in other forums, participants at this one clearly identified the roles that university and college administrators must play in recognizing and responding to the challenges of standards-based experiences that incoming students increasingly will bring to the institutions. Participants looked to deans and provosts as the academic leaders in higher education to accept the charge of responding and to respond, in part, by using introductory and other required SME&T courses as the starting point for more encompassing systemic changes in SME&T education. (It is important to note that most faculty remarked that the message to improve undergraduate teaching must come from university administration, while conversely, deans and provosts commented that, ultimately, faculty controlled the classroom environment. This strongly suggests that more effective communication is essential between faculty and administrators about expectations, strategies, and goals for teaching at the postsecondary level.)

This forum's discussions helped to inform the development of **Visions 1**, **2**, **3**, and **5** in this report.

Topical Forums: Conclusion

The topical forums offered important opportunities for the members of CUSE to build upon the momentum of the national convocation held in 1995 and the subsequent regional symposia. In collaboration with professional organizations and universities and, in one case, with a state department of education, CUSE members were able to explore with colleagues across the United States issues that were raised at the regional symposia. For example, strategies for developing and implementing interdisciplinary courses—prominent topics in the first symposium at the University of Michigan—were subsequently revisited at the two topical forums held in collaboration with the NCTM and the University of Washington System.

The topical forums also enabled committee members to engage diverse stakeholders in conversations about particularly challenging and complicated topics. These included increasing scientific literacy for all undergraduate students, improving the preparation of future K-12 teachers in science and mathematics, and identifying how to overcome professional and institutional obstacles that faculty face in improving their teaching skills.

APPENDIX B

INSTITUTIONS AND ORGANIZATIONS REPRESENTED AT THE REGIONAL SYMPOSIA AND TOPICAL FORUMS

Addison-Wesley Publishing Company, Reading, MA

Adrian College, Adrian, MI

Advanced Information Microstructures, Acton, MA

Albion College, Albion, MI

American Association of University Women, Northville, MI

American Geophysical Union, Washington, DC

American Mathematical Society, Washington, DC

American Mathematical Society, Providence, RI

American River College, Sacramento, CA

American Society of Limnology and Oceanography, Washington, DC

Amoco Corporation, Chicago, IL

Ann Arbor Public Schools, Ann Arbor, MI

ARETE Technologies, Inc., Harvard, MA

Arizona State University, Tempe, AZ

Arkansas State University, Jonesboro, AR

ASARCO Inc., New York, NY

Azusa Pacific University, Azusa, CA

Baker College, Flint, MI

Barry University, Miami Shores, FL

Baylor College of Medicine, Waco, TX

Belleview High School, Belleview, FL

Berry College, Mount Berry, GA

Bethune-Cookman College, Daytona Beach, FL

Bloomfield Hills Schools, Bloomfield, MI

Boeing Company, Seattle, WA

Boston College, Chestnut Hill, MA

Boston University, Boston, MA

Bowdoin College, Brunswick, ME

Bowling Green High School, Bowling Green, MO

Brandeis University, Waltham, MA

Brevard Community College, Cocoa, FL

Brevard Community College, Melbourne, FL

Bridgewater State College, Bridgewater, MA

Brigham Young University, Provo, UT

Broward Community College, Davie, FL

Broward Community College - North Campus, Coconut Creek, FL

Broward Community College, Pembroke, FL

Brown University, Providence, RI

Bryn Mawr College, Bryn Mawr, PA

Buchholz High School, Gainesville, FL

Cabrillo College, Aptos, CA

California Institute of Technology, Pasadena, CA

California Lutheran University, Thousand Oaks, CA

California State Polytechnic University, Pomona, CA

California State Polytechnic University, San Luis Obispo, CA

California State University, Bakersfield, CA

California State University, Carson City, CA

California State University, Dominguez Hills, CA

California State University, Fresno, CA

California State University, Fullerton, CA

California State University, Long Beach, CA

California State University, Los Angeles, CA

California State University, Monterey Bay, CA

California State University, San Bernardino, CA

California State University, San Marcos, CA

Center for American Archeology, Kampsville, IL

Center for Educational Equity in Mathematics, Science, and Technology, California State Polytechnic Institute, Pomona, CA

Central Connecticut State University, New Britain, CT

Central Florida Community College, Boca Raton, FL

Central Florida Community College, Ocala, FL

Central Michigan University, Mt. Pleasant, MI

Central Washington University, Ellensburg, WA

Centralia College, Centralia, WA

Chadwick School, Palos Verdes, CA

Chaparral Middle School, Diamond Bar, CA

Chapman College, Orange, CA

Cheesebrough-Pond's USA Company, Trumbull, CT

Chevron Chemical Company, Houston, TX

Chevron Chemical Company, Kingwood, TX

Chipola Junior College, Marianna, FL

Chippewa Valley High School, Mt. Clemens, MI

CIA Laboratories, St. Joseph, MO

City University of New York, New York, NY

City University of New York - Kingsborough, Brooklyn, NY

City University of New York, Medgar Evers College, Brooklyn, NY

Claremont Graduate School, Claremont, CA

Clark Atlanta University, Atlanta, GA

Clemson University, Clemson, SC

Coastal Carolina University, Conway, SC

Colby College, Waterville, ME

College of Staten Island, Staten Island, NY

College of William and Mary, Williamsburg, VA

Colorado State University, Fort Collins, CO

Columbia University, New York, NY

Columbus State University, Columbus, GA

Connecticut Academy for Education in Mathematics, Science, & Technology, Middletown, CT

Connecticut State Department of Education, Hartford, CT

Cornell University, Ithaca, NY

Cummer Museum, Jacksonville, FL

Curry College, Milton, MA

Cypress College, Cypress, CA

Dartmouth College, Hanover, NH

Daytona Beach Community College, Daytona Beach, FL

Delta State University, Cleveland, MS

Dickinson College, Carlisle, PA

Digital Equipment Corporation, Acton, MA

Digital Equipment Corporation, Littleton, MA

Dow Chemical Company, Midland, MI

Drexel University, Philadelphia, PA

Duval County Public Schools, Jacksonville, FL

Eastern Kentucky University, Richmond, KY

Eastern Michigan University, Ypsilanti, MI

Eastern Washington University, Cheney, WA

East Los Angeles College, Monterey Park, CA

Edison Community College, Ft. Myers, FL

Edmonds Community College, Lynnwood, WA

Education Development Center, Newton, MA

Edward Waters College, Jacksonville, FL

Eli Lilly and Company, Indianapolis, IN

Emerson School, Ann Arbor, MI

Endicott College, Beverly, MA

Everett Community College, Everett, WA

Evergreen State College, Olympia, WA

Exxon Company USA, Houston, TX

Exxon Education Foundation, Irving, TX

Fairfield University, Fairfield, CT

Ferris State University, Big Rapids, MI

Fitchburg State College, Fitchburg, MA

Flinders University, Adelaide, Australia

Florida A&M University, Tallahassee, FL

Florida Atlantic University, Boca Raton, FL

Florida Department of Education, Tallahassee, FL

Florida DOE Area Center for Educational Enhancement, Boca Raton, FL

Florida Gulf Coast University, Ft. Myers, Fl

Florida Institute of Education, Jacksonville, FL

Florida Institute of Technology, Melbourne, FL

Florida International University, Miami, FL

Florida State University, Tallahassee, FL

Ford Motor Company, Dearborn, MI

Ft. McCoy K-8 School, Ft. McCoy, FL

Franklin & Marshall College, Lancaster, PA

Fred Hutchinson Cancer Research Center, Seattle, WA

Fresno Pacific College, Fresno, CA

Fugro-McClelland (Southwest), Inc., Houston, TX

General Atomics, San Diego, CA

GeoForschungsZentrum, Potsdam, Germany

George J. Ball, Inc., Chicago, IL

Georgia State University, Atlanta, GA

Georgia Technical University, Atlanta, GA

Gettysburg College, Gettysburg, PA

Glendale Community College, Glendale, CA

GMI Engineering & Management Institute Flint, MI

Golforest Elementary School, Houston, TX

Grand Valley State University, Allendale, MI

Grossmont Union High School District, La Mesa, CA

GTE Foundation, Stamford, CT

GTE Laboratories, Waltham, MA

Gulf Coast Community College, Panama City, FL

Hamilton College, Clinton, NY

Harbor Branch Oceanography, Ft. Pierce, FL

Harvard Graduate School of Education, Woburn, MA

Harvard-Smithsonian Center for Astrophysics, Cambridge, MA

Harvard University, Cambridge, MA

Harvey Mudd College, Claremont, CA

Henry Ford Health System, Detroit, MI

Heublein, Inc., Hartford, CT

Highline Community College, Des Moines, WA

Hillsborough Community College, Tampa, FL

Hillsborough County Schools, Tampa, FL

Hope College, Holland, MI

Houston Baptist University, Houston, TX

Howard Hughes Medical Institute, Chevy Chase, MD

Howmet Corporation, Whitehall, MI

ICF Kaiser Consulting Group, Saline, MI

Ida High School, Saline, MI

Indiana State University, Terre Haute, IN

Indiana University, Bloomington, IN

Indiana University-Purdue University of Indiana, Indianapolis, IN

International Thomson Publishers, Missouri City, TX

Inverness Research, Los Angeles, CA

Jacksonville Community College - Downtown Campus, Jacksonville, FL

Jacksonville Community College - Kent Campus, Jacksonville, FL

Jacksonville Community College - North Campus, Jacksonville, FL

Jacksonville Community College - South Campus, Jacksonville, FL

Jacksonville Museum of History, Jacksonville, FL

Jacksonville University, Jacksonville, FL

James Madison University, Harrisonburg, VA

Jeff L. Bott Investments, Stafford, TX

Johnson Controls, Inc., Milwaukee, WI

Kanapaha Middle School, Gainesville, FL

Kansas State University, Manhattan, KS

King/Drew High School of Medicine & Science, Los Angeles, CA

King Philip Middle School, West Hartford, CT

Krug Life Sciences, Inc., Houston, TX

LA Collaborative for Teacher Excellence, Los Angeles, CA

Lake City Community College, Lake City, FL

Lake-Sumter Community College, Leesburg, FL

Lamont-Doherty Earth Observatory, Columbia Univ., Palisades, NY

Lansing Community College, Lansing, MI

LaSalle University, Philadelphia, PA

Lawrence Technological University, Southfield, MI

Lexington Community College, Lexington, KY

Loral Space Information Systems, Houston, TX

Louisiana State University, Baton Rouge, LA

Loyola Marymount University, Los Angeles, CA

Loyola University, New Orleans, LA

Manatee Community College, Bradenton, FL

Marion County School Board, Ocala, FL

Massachusetts College of Art, Jamaica Plains, MA

Massachusetts Department of Education, Malden, MA

Massachusetts Institute of Technology, Cambridge, MA

Massachusetts Institute of Technology, Westford, MA

Massasoit Community College, Brockton, MA

Master's College, The, Newhall, CA

McDonnell Douglas Aerospace, Houston, TX

McMaster University, Hamilton, Ontario

Mesa Community College, Mesa, AZ

Miami-Dade Community College, Miami, FL

Miami University, Middletown, OH

Michigan Chamber of Commerce, Ann Arbor, MI

Michigan State University, East Lansing, MI

Michigan State University, Laingsburg, MI

Middlesex Community College, Bedford, MA

MITRE Corporation, Bedford, MA

Mitsubishi Electric Research Laboratories, Inc., Cambridge, MA

Moorpark College, Moorpark, CA

Morehouse College, Atlanta, GA

Motorola, Inc., Schaumburg, IL

Mount Holyoke College, Houston, TX

Murray State University, Murray, KY

Muskegon Community College, Muskegon, MI

National Aeronautics and Space Administration, Houston, TX

National Center for Atmospheric Research, Boulder, CO

National Council of Teachers of Mathematics, Reston, VA

National Science Foundation, Arlington, VA

National Science Teachers Association, Arlington, VA

Naval Research Laboratory, Stennis Space Center, MS

Naval Undersea Warfare Center, Newport, RI

North East Florida Educational Consortium, Palatka, FL

New York City Technical College, Brooklyn, NY

Nissan Technical Center, Farmington Hills, MI

North Carolina State University, Raleigh, NC

Northeastern University, Boston, MA

Northern Illinois University, DeKalb, IL

North Florida Junior College, Madison, FL

North Harris College, Houston, TX

North Seattle Community College, Seattle, WA

Northwestern University, Evanston, IL

Norwood Elementary School, St. Petersburg, FL

Nova Southeastern University, Ft. Lauderdale, FL

Oakland Community College - Royal Oak Campus, Royal Oak, MI

Oak Ridge National Laboratory, Oak Ridge, TN

Occidental College, Los Angeles, CA

Office of the Commissioner for Education, Miami, FL

OHM Remediation Services Corporation, Trenton, NJ

Oklahoma State University, Norman, OK

Old Dominion University, Richmond, VA

Olin Research Center, Cheshire, CT

Orange Coast College, Costa Mesa, CA

Okaloosa-Walton Community College, Niceville, FL

Pacific Lutheran University, Tacoma, WA

Pacific Northwest Laboratories, Richland, WA

Pacific Science Center, Seattle, WA

Palm Beach Community College, Boca Raton, FL

Palm Beach Community College - Central Campus, Lake Worth, FL

Palm Beach Community College - Glades Campus, Belle Glade, FL

Palm Beach Community College - North Campus, Palm Beach Gardens, FL

Palomar College, San Marcos, CA

Parke-Davis Pharmaceuticals Division, Ann Arbor, MI

Pasco County Schools, Land O'Lakes, FL

Pasco-Hernando Community College, New Port Richey, FL

Pennsylvania State University, University Park, PA

Pepperdine University, Malibu, CA

Pfizer Central Research, Groton, CT

Pfizer, Inc., Groton, CT

Philadelphia College of Pharmacy and Science, Philadelphia, PA

Physics Today, Santa Barbara, CA

Pierce College, Lakewood, WA

Point Loma Nazarene College, San Diego, CA

Pomona College, Claremont, CA

Portland Community College, Portland, OR

Portland State University, Portland, OR

Prairie View A&M, Prairie View, TX

Praxair, Inc., Danbury, CT

Princeton University, Princeton, NJ

Project Kaleidoscope, Washington, DC

Providence College, Providence, RI

Purdue North Central, Westville, IN

PWS Publishing, Boston, MA

Queens College of CUNY, Queens, NY

Queen's University, Kingston, Ontario

Raa Middle School, Tallahassee, FL

Raytheon Company, Lexington, MA

Rensselaer Polytechnic Institute, Troy, NY

Rice University, Houston, TX

RMD, Inc., Watertown, MA

Robert A. Welch Foundation, The, Houston, TX

Rochester Institute of Technology, Rochester, NY

Rockwell International, Seal Beach, CA

Rollins College, Winter Park, FL

Rose-Hulman Institute of Technology, Terre Haute, IN

Rutgers University, Newark, NJ

S. C. Johnson & Son Inc., Racine, WI

Saint Joseph College, West Hartford, CT

Saint Leo College, Saint Leo, FL

Saint Mary's College, Notre Dame, IN

Saint Michael's College, Colchester, VT

Sam Houston State University, Huntsville, TX

Sam Rayburn Junior College, Bryan, TX

San Bernardino County Office of Education, San Bernardino, CA

San Diego State University, San Diego, CA

San Francisco State University, San Francisco, CA

San Jacinto College, Pasadena, TX

San Jose State University, San Jose, CA

Santa Fe Community College, Gainesville, FL

Santa Monica College, Santa Monica, CA

Schoolcraft College, Northville, MI

Science Magazine, Los Angeles, CA

Sealey Elementary School, Tallahassee, FL

Seattle Central Community College, Seattle, WA

Seattle University, Seattle, WA

Seminole Community College, Sanford, FL

Shady Hill Elementary School, Ocala, FL

Shell Oil Company, Houston, TX

Simmons College, Boston, MA

Skagit Valley College, Mt. Vernon, WA

Society of Environmental Toxicology and Chemistry, Washington, DC

Sonoma State University, Rohnert Park, CA

South Florida Community College, Avon Park, FL

Southern Methodist University, Dallas, TX

South Seattle Community College, Seattle, WA

Southwest Research Institute, San Antonio, TX

Southwest Texas State College, San Marco, TX

Space Center Houston, Houston, TX

Square D Company, Palatine, IL

SRI International, Menlo Park, CA

St. Edward's University, Austin, TX

St. Petersburg Junior College-Community College, Clearwater, FL

St. Thomas University, Miami, FL

Stanford University, Stanford, CA

Stanton College Preparatory School, Jacksonville, FL

State University of New York, Oswego, NY

State University of New York, Stony Brook, NY

State University System of Florida, Miami, FL

Stetson University, Deland, FL

Swarthmore College, Swarthmore, PA

Tallahassee Community College, Tallahassee, FL

TAV Associates, Boston, MA

Temple University, Philadelphia, PA

Texas A&M University, College Station, TX

Texas A&M University, Galveston, TX

Texas A&M University, Kingsville, TX

Texas Southern University, Houston, TX

Texas Tech University, Lubbock, TX

Texas Wesleyan University, Fort Worth, TX

The Union Institute, North Miami, FL

Trinity College, Washington, DC

Trinity University, San Antonio, TX

TRW Space & Electronics Group, Redondo Beach, CA

Tufts University, Medford, MA

Unidata, UCAR, Boulder, CO

Union Carbide Corporation, Danbury, CT

U.S. Coast Guard Academy, New London, CT

U.S. Environmental Protection Agency, Washington, DC

United Technologies Corporation, Hartford, CT

Universities Space Research Association, Whitelaw, WI

University of Akron, Akron, OH

University of Alabama, Tuscaloosa, AL

University of Arizona, Tucson, AZ

University of California, Berkeley, CA

University of California, Davis, CA

University of California, Irvine, CA

University of California, Los Angeles, CA

University of California, Riverside, CA

University of California, San Diego, CA

University of California, Santa Barbara, CA

University of California, Santa Cruz, CA

University of California, San Diego, La Jolla, CA

University of Central Arkansas, Conway, AR

University of Central Florida, Orlando, FL

University of Chicago, Chicago, IL

University of Connecticut, Storrs, CT

University of Delaware, Newark, DE

University of Detroit, Detroit, MI

University of Detroit, Mercy, Detroit, MI

University of Florida, Gainesville, FL

University of Georgia, Athens, GA

University of Houston, Clear Lake, TX

University of Houston, Houston, TX

University of Houston, Victoria, TX

University of Idaho, Moscow, ID

University of La Verne, La Verne, CA

University of Maryland, College Park, MD

University of Massachusetts, Amherst, MA

University of Massachusetts - Dartmouth, N. Dartmouth, MA

University of Massachusetts - Lowell, Lowell, MA

University of Miami, Coral Gables, FL

University of Michigan, Allen Park, MI

University of Michigan, Ann Arbor, MI

University of Michigan, Dearborn, MI

University of Michigan, Flint, MI

University of Michigan, Lincoln Park, MI

University of Minnesota, Minneapolis, MN

University of Missouri, Columbia, MO

University of Missouri, St. Louis, MO

University of North Carolina, Chapel Hill, Chapel Hill, NC

University of Northern Iowa, Cedar Falls, IA

University of North Florida, Jacksonville, FL

University of Oklahoma, Norman, OK

University of Pennsylvania, Philadelphia, PA

University of Puget Sound, Tacoma, WA

University of Quebec, Montreal, Quebec

University of Redlands, Redlands, CA

University of San Diego, San Diego, CA

University of South Carolina, Spartanburg, SC

University of South Dakota, Vermillion, SD

University of South Florida, St. Petersburg, FL

University of South Florida, Tampa, FL

University of Southern California, Los Angeles, CA

University of Tennessee, Knoxville, TN

University of Tennessee, Martin, TN

University of Texas, Arlington, TX

University of Texas, Austin, TX

University of Texas, Brownsville, TX

University of Texas, Dallas, TX

University of Texas, Edinburg, TX

University of Texas, El Paso, TX

University of Texas, Houston Health Sciences Center, Houston, TX

University of Texas, Pan American, TX

University of Texas, Permian Basin, TX

University of Texas, Richardson, TX

University of Texas, San Antonio, TX

University of Texas, Tyler, TX

University of the Pacific, Stockton, CA

University of Washington System, Seattle, WA

University of West Florida, Tallahassee, FL

University of West Florida, Pensacola, FL

University of Wisconsin, Madison, WI

Upjohn Company, Kalamazoo, MI

Upjohn Laboratories, Kalamazoo, MI

U.S. Air Force, Rome Laboratories, Hanscom Air Force Base, MA

Valencia Community College, Orlando, FL

Vanderbilt University, Nashville, TN

Vanderbilt University Medical Center, Nashville, TN

Virginia Polytechnical Institute & State University, Blacksburg, VA

Warner Southern College, Lake Wales, FL

Washington State University, Pullman, WA

Wastenaw Community College, Chelsea, MI

Wayne County Community College - Downtown Campus, Detroit, MI

Wayne County Community College - Eastern Campus, Detroit, MI

Wellesley College, Wellesley, MA

Wesleyan University, Middletown, CT

West Los Angeles College, Culver City, CA

West Virginia University, Morgantown, WV

Western Connecticut State University, Danbury, CT

Western Michigan University Kalamazoo, MI

Western New England College, Springfield, MA

Western Washington University, Bellingham, WA

Western Washington University, Port Angeles, WA

Westreco, Inc., New Milford, CT

Whatcom Community College, Bellingham, WA

Wheaton College, Norton, MA

Whittier College, Whittier, CA

Williams College ,Williamstown, MA

Woodrow Wilson Elementary School, Manhattan, KS

Worcester Polytechnic Institute, Worcester, MA

Wright State University, Dayton, OH

Xerox Corporation, Stamford, CT

Yale University, New Haven, CT

Zephyrhills High School, Zephyrhills, FL

APPENDIX C

BIOGRAPHICAL SKETCHES OF MEMBERS OF THE COMMITTEE ON UNDERGRADUATE SCIENCE EDUCATION (CUSE)

Current Members

Marye Anne Fox (NAS*), *North Carolina State University and CUSE Chair,* is Chancellor of North Carolina State University in Raleigh, NC. Prior to assuming the Chancellorship position, Dr. Fox was Vice President for Research and the M. June and J. Virgil Waggoner Regents Chair in Chemistry at the University of Texas at Austin. Her recent research activities include organic photochemistry, electrochemistry, and physical organic mechanisms. She is a former associate editor of the *Journal of the American Chemical Society*. Previously, she was the director of the Center for Fast Kinetics Research, vice chair of the National Science Board, and a member of the Task Force on Alternative Futures for the Department of Energy National Laboratories, the Galvin Committee. Dr. Fox is a member of the National Academy of Sciences and serves on several NAS and NRC committees. In addition to her role as Chair of the Committee on Undergraduate Science Education, she serves on the NAS Council Executive Committee and the Committee on Science, Engineering, and Public Policy. Dr. Fox is a former member of the Commission on Physical Sciences, Mathematics, and Applications and served on the Committee on Criteria for Federal Support of Research and Development. She received a Ph.D. in organic chemistry from Dartmouth College.

*NAS: Member of the National Academy of Sciences

Mary P. Colvard, *Cobleskill-Richmondville High School,* is a biology and research teacher at Cobleskill-Richmondville High School in Cobleskill, New York. She has taught there for the past eight years and prior to that was for 20 years a science teacher and department chair at Sidney High School. Ms. Colvard presently serves as Region II Coordinator for the National Association of Biology Teachers and Director at Large for Biology for the Science Teachers Association of New York State. She is also a member of the board of directors of the Health, Safety, and Research Alliance for New York State. Other professional affiliations include membership in the American Society for Microbiology and the National Science Teachers Association. Ms. Colvard has authored many labs for the Howard Hughes Medical Institute-funded Cornell Institute for Biology Teachers and has served as a summer instructor for the program. She has been a contributing author to several high school science textbooks. Ms. Colvard received a B.S.Ed in biology from the State University of New York at Geneseo and her M.S.Ed in secondary biology from the State University of New York at Oneonta. She has completed additional graduate work at Binghamton University and Cornell University.

Arthur B. Ellis, *University of Wisconsin, Madison,* is Meloche-Bascom Professor of Chemistry at the University of Wisconsin, Madison. He conducts research in the inter- disciplinary field of materials science and has led an effort to develop instructional materials for integrating this field into the chemistry curriculum. Dr. Ellis leads the College Level One Team of the National Science Foundation-supported National Institute for Science Education (NISE), which is examining ways to make introductory college science, mathematics, engineering and technology courses more effective. He also serves on the Committee on Undergraduate Science Education of the National Research Council. Dr. Ellis received a B.S. in chemistry from Caltech in 1973, and his Ph.D. degree in inorganic chemistry from MIT in 1977.

Dorothy Gabel, *Indiana University,* is a professor in the School of Education at Indiana University and the coordinator of science education. She presently teaches and supervises a required introductory science course for prospective elementary teachers entitled "Introduction to Scientific Inquiry." Dr. Gabel's specialty is in chemistry education, and she is the author of numerous research papers in this area and of a high school chemistry text. She was the editor of *The Handbook of Research on Science Teaching and Learning* and has served as president of the Hoosier Science Teachers Association, the School Science and Mathematics Association, and the National Association for Research in Science Teaching Association.

James M. Gentile, *Hope College,* received a B.A. in biology from St. Mary's College (MN) in 1968, and his M.S. (1970) and Ph.D. (1974) degrees in genetics from Illinois State University. From 1974-1976 he worked as a postdoctoral research associate in the Department of Human Genetics at the Yale University School of Medicine. He was appointed assistant professor of biology at Hope College in 1976 and was promoted to associate professor in 1982 and to full professor in 1984. In 1984 Dr. Gentile was also awarded an endowed chair and distinguished scholar position in the biological sciences at Hope College, an honor he holds to this day. Dr. Gentile also twice held appointments as

adjunct professor of genetics at the University of Illinois (1983-84; 1985-86). In 1986, Dr. Gentile was appointed chair of the biology department at Hope College, and in 1988 he was appointed to his present position as dean for the natural sciences at Hope College. Dr. Gentile's research investigates ways in which plant and animal cells metabolize xenobiotic agents into forms that can cause mutations in host or target cells. His current research efforts are focused on ways infectious agents work to enhance neoplastic risk in mammalian organisms. Since 1976 over 100 undergraduate students have conducted research with Dr. Gentile. He has authored or co-authored 65 peer-reviewed publications since 1973. Dr. Gentile has a long listing of honors and special appointments. He has been a panelist for the NIH/NTP three times (1985-88; 1989-91; 1996-98) a consultant to a WHO Advisory Group (1983-85), a NIEHS Superfund panelist (1987-89) and a team leader for an internal NIOSH review panel (1990). Dr. Gentile has also served on an International Committee for the Protection Against Environmental Mutagens and Carcinogens Task Force (1986-91), an International Agency for Research on Cancer Panel (1995), and as a consultant to the USEPA Science Advisory Board (1988-95). He has served as a consultant to over 50 academic institutions in the past 20 years, as a consultant to 10 different industries since 1980, and is a science consultant to the Murdock Trust. Dr. Gentile is a member of the executive committee of Project Kaleidoscope (PKAL), an NSF-sponsored national organization focused on enhancing science and mathematics education in the U.S. and he has served as an elected councilor for the Council on Undergraduate Research (CUR). He was chair of the Program Committee for the 1993 annual meeting of the Environmental Mutagen Society (EMS) and has served as president of the society (1993-95). Dr. Gentile was the book review editor for the journal *Environmental and Molecular Mutagenesis,* and has served on the editorial review board for that journal, for *Revista Genetica,* the *CUR Newsletter,* and *Mutation Research.* Dr. Gentile is currently the managing editor of *Mutation Research: Fundamental and Molecular Mechanisms of Mutations* and executive managing editor of *Mutation Research.*

Ronald J. Henry, *Georgia State University,* is the provost and vice president for Academic Affairs at Georgia State University (since July, 1994). One of his responsibilities is to develop Georgia State into a premier urban research university. Another responsibility is leadership to promote and recommend changes in public education systems that will improve student success at all levels, pre-school through post-secondary (P-16) education, and into the world of work. Previously, he served as chief academic officer for Miami University (Ohio) and Auburn University. Dr. Henry serves as a member of the Georgia P-16 Council. He served as an evaluator on the 1995 Education Pilot Evaluation Team of the Malcolm Baldrige National Quality Award and as an Examiner on the 1996 Board of Examiners. Dr. Henry received B.Sc. and Ph.D. degrees in applied mathematics from Queen's University, Belfast, in 1961 and 1964, respectively.

Harvey B. Keynes, *University of Minnesota,* is a professor of mathematics, past director of education in the Geometry Center, and director of the (science/engineering school) Institute of Technology Center for Educational Programs. His research interests are in dynamical systems and mathematics education. Professor Keynes directs the following projects: The University of Minnesota Talented Youth Mathematics Program, (UMTYMP—state and private funding); the National Science Foundation Mathematicians and Education Reform Network; the NSF Young Scholars Project; the Bush Foundation Project to increase female participation in UMTYMP; the NSF-funded Early Alert Initiative; and a new reformed calculus program for University of Minnesota engineering

students. Professor Keynes also has taught in the University of Minnesota Talented Youth Program and has developed a new masters program in mathematics that includes secondary teaching certification. He has extensive contacts in Minnesota and national mathematics education and high technology committees, as well as membership in committees of major mathematics organizations and projects. He was a member of the NRC's Mathematical Sciences Education Board and is the recipient of the 1992 Award for Distinguished Public Service of the American Mathematical Society. Professor Keynes obtained his B.S. and M.A. degrees in mathematics from the University of Pennsylvania in 1962/63 and his Ph.D. in mathematics from Wesleyan University in 1966.

Paul J. Kuerbis, *The Colorado College,* is a professor of education at The Colorado College in Colorado Springs. He has been at the college since 1973 and teaches in both the elementary and secondary licensure programs. He founded and directs the Master of Arts in Teaching Secondary Science program that leads to Colorado licensure and the Master of Arts in Teaching Integrated Natural Sciences program for experienced teachers. From 1989-92, he was director of curriculum and instruction for the National Center for Improving Science Education (NCISE), funded initially by the U.S. Department of Education. He is the current past president of the Association for the Education of Teachers in Science (AETS) and serves on the editorial board of the *Journal of Science Teacher Education.* He was a member of the National Research Council's (NRC) working group on science teaching standards and a contributing author to the *National Science Education Standards.* Professor Kuerbis received his B.A. in biology from St. Mary's College (California) in 1964, his masters in zoology from U.C.L.A. in 1966, and his Ph.D. in science education from the University of California, Berkeley (1976). He has taught science at the middle, high school, and community college levels, and at The Colorado College.

R. Heather Macdonald, *College of William and Mary,* is associate professor of geology at the College of William and Mary, where she recently served as dean of Undergraduate Studies, Arts and Sciences. She is a past-president of the National Association of Geoscience Teachers (NAGT) and currently co-coordinates NAGT workshops on innovative and effective teaching in the geosciences. She also serves on the education committee of the Geological Society of America and the K-12 Earth Science Education Committee of the Society for Sedimentary Geology. She received the Biggs Earth Science Teaching Award from the Geological Society of America and the Thomas Jefferson Teaching Award from the College of William and Mary. Dr. Macdonald received a B.A. in geology from Carleton College in 1976 and her M.S. and Ph.D. degrees in geology from the University of Wisconsin, Madison, in 1979 and 1984, respectively.

Edward E. Penhoet, *Chiron Corporation,* is President and CEO of Chiron. He is a leader in the field of biotechnology. He has been CEO of Chiron since co-founding the company in 1981. From 1971-1981, Dr. Penhoet was a faculty member of the biochemistry department at the University of California, Berkeley, and continues as an adjunct. He also is a member of the Scientific Advisory Board to the U.S. Congress and has testified regarding the biotechnology industry and the role of federal funding in support of basic research.

Grace McWhorter, *Lawson State Community College,* was named chairperson of the Natural Science Department of Lawson State Community College in 1993. She is project site director for the Biomedical Bridge to the Baccalaureate Degree Program. Funding from the National Institutes of Health supports this project. She serves as chair of the State of Alabama's Master Teacher Plan and is chair for chemistry on the State Articulation Committee. Dr. McWhorter has played a key role in the planning and development of the state's Teaching and Learning Symposium

(1995-1998). Dr. McWhorter is the recipient of several prestigious awards, including the Distinguished Service Award from Florida A&M University; Outstanding Alumnus Award in Agriculture from Tuskegee University; and the Chancellor's Award for Outstanding Faculty from the Alabama College System. Prior to joining the faculty at Lawson State, Dr. McWhorter was a faculty member at several institutions, including the University of Missouri at St. Louis, Jacksonville State University, and the University of Texas at San Antonio. Dr. McWhorter received both B.S. and M.S. degrees in horticulture/plant and soil science from Tuskegee Institute (University). She earned her Ph.D. in plant pathology/botany from the University of Florida in 1978 and the Master of Divinity from Besson Divinity School at Samford University in 1992. She is a member of the Alabama Academy of Science and the National Association of Biology Teachers.

James W. Serum, *Hewlett-Packard Company,* is a senior scientist for Hewlett-Packard Company in the Chemical Analysis Group in Wilmington, Delaware. In this capacity, he is responsible for exploration of advanced technologies for chemical measurement systems. He has held numerous scientific and management positions during his 24 years at HP, including group R&D manager and general manager of Scientific Instruments Division. Dr. Serum serves on a variety of scientific and educational boards and National Research Council committees, including, the committee for the National Digital Library, and the panel for Chemical Science and Technology (NIST). In addition, he is a member of the board of advisors for the Center for Photochemical Sciences at Bowling Green State University. Dr. Serum received a B.A. in chemistry from Hope College and a Ph.D. degree in organic chemistry from the University of Colorado.

Elaine Seymour, *University of Colorado, Boulder,* is the director of ethnography and evaluation research in the Bureau of

Sociological Research, the University of Colorado, Boulder. She has also served as senior scientist at the National Institute for Science Education, the University of Madison, Wisconsin, as a member of the "College Level One" team. The work of her research unit is mainly concerned with aspects of change in the education and career paths of undergraduate and graduate science, mathematics, and engineering (SME) majors. Recent research includes a major national study of reasons why SME undergraduates leave the sciences and special studies of women, students of color, and students with disabilities in these fields. She is the co-evaluator of two NSF consortia for the reform of undergraduate chemistry (shared with the University of California, Berkeley), with a focus on the processes of change among students, faculty, and departments. This work has led to cross-initiative work, including the development of a field-tested web-site collection of student learning assessment tools developed by and for faculty involved in the reform of curriculum and pedagogy. Dr. Seymour offers evaluation workshops and consulting for a number of other SME education reform initiatives. She has over 30 years of experience in teaching, curriculum development, research, and evaluation. Her undergraduate honours degree (in economics and political science) was awarded by the University of Keele, England, a masters of education by the University of Glasgow, Scotland, and her Ph.D. in sociology (with a specialty in medical sociology) by the University of Colorado, Boulder.

Christy Vogel, *Cabrillo College,* is a chemistry instructor at Cabrillo College, a community college located on the Central Coast of California. Her experience with undergraduate science education began at Fort Lewis College, a four-year college in Colorado. In the process of obtaining her B.S. in chemistry, she was employed as a lab assistant, departmental tutor, and summer research assistant at Fort Lewis College. This positive experience with both teaching and research

as an undergraduate inspired her to continue her education at the University of Southern California, where she received her Ph.D. in physical chemistry in 1990. Upon completion of her doctoral degree, Dr. Vogel returned to teaching. She enjoys teaching at a community college because it is an opportunity to return what she received as an undergraduate— science education that is affordable, competitive, and personal. Dr. Vogel has participated in programs such as CAMPS and MESA and is currently the faculty adviser for ACCESS. All of these programs are dedicated to increasing diversity in the sciences. She is one of the authors of the American Chemical Society's standardized General Chemistry I exam (1996). Her current projects include small-scale laboratory experiments and developing an "Art in Chemistry" course for non-science majors.

David Wilkinson (NAS*), *Princeton University.* After a brief lectureship at the University of Michigan, Dr. Wilkinson moved to Princeton in 1963, becoming a professor of physics in 1972. He chaired the Physics Department from 1987 to 1990. Early in his career, he received a Sloan Foundation fellowship and a Guggenheim fellowship. He is a member of the National Academy of Sciences, a fellow of the American Physical Society, and a member of the American Astronomical Society. His research interests include gravitation and relativity, primeval galaxies, and cosmic microwave radiation. He was a principal researcher for the Cosmic Background Explorer (COBE) and a member of the Microwave Anisotropy Project (MAP) team.

Former Members†

C. Bradley Moore (NAS*), *University of California, Berkeley, and Past CUSE Chair,* is professor of chemistry at the University of California at Berkeley and director of the

---

†These former members of CUSE participated in the development of this report and have approved its contents.

Chemical Sciences Division at the Lawrence Berkeley Laboratory. He also has served as chair of the Department of Chemistry and dean of the College of Chemistry at Berkeley. His many research interests include molecular energy transfer, the dynamics of chemical reactions, photochemistry, and spectroscopy. His research, including pioneering work on vibrational energy transfer among the modes of polyatomic molecules using laser methods, was recognized by the National Academy of Sciences, where he has been a member since 1986. His research also has been recognized by prizes and awards from the American Physical Society and the American Photochemical Society. He is the editor of *Chemical and Biochemical Applications of Lasers* and a member of the editorial board for *Laser Chemistry*. Dr. Moore has served on numerous disciplinary and education committees and boards of the National Research Council. His service to chemistry committees has included the Panel for Chemical Physics; the Committee on Atomic, Molecular, and Optical Sciences; and the AFOSR Chemical Sciences Review Panel. Committee assignments in education include the CUSE (chair from the committee's inception in 1993 until 1997), the advisory board to the NRC's Center for Science, Mathematics, and Engineering Education, the Committee on Information Technology, and the working group on Science Content Standards for the *National Science Education Standards*. Dr. Moore received his B.A. from Harvard University and his Ph.D. from the University of California at Berkeley.

Isaac Abella, *University of Chicago,* is professor of physics at the University of Chicago. His field is non-linear optical physics, ultrafast transient phenomena, and laser interactions in atoms and ions in solids. He received a B.A. in physics and astronomy from the University of Toronto, and M.A. and Ph.D. in Physics from Columbia University, where he worked under Professor Charles H. Townes. He has been a fellow at the Joint Institute for Laboratory Astrophysics in Boulder,

Colorado; visiting scientist at the Optical Sciences Division, Naval Research Laboratory, Washington, DC; guest scientist at National Bureau of Standards (NIST), Time & Frequency Division, Boulder Labs; and research fellow at Argonne National Laboratory. He has served as a member of the Education Committee of the American Physical Society; chair of Education Committee of Laser Science Topical Group, (APS); chair, Isaakson Prize Committee, American Physical Society (APS); and member of the National Science Standards Working Group of the National Research Council. He is a fellow of the APS and of the Optical Society of America and president of the Chicago Chapter of Sigma Xi. He was awarded the Quantrell Prize for Excellence in Undergraduate Teaching at Chicago. He is the resident master of the largest college residence hall at the University of Chicago.

Neal Abraham, *DePauw University,* is Vice-President for Academic Affairs and Dean of Faculty. He was the Rachel C. Hale Professor of the Sciences and Mathematics and Professor of Physics at Bryn Mawr College. A fellow of the American Physical Society, Optical Society of America, and the American Association for the Advancement of Science, with research interests in laser physics and nonlinear dynamics, Dr. Abraham has been actively involved in science education reform through the American Association of Physics Teachers, the Association of American Colleges, and Project Kaleidoscope (since its inception in 1989). Dr. Abraham coordinated regional PKAL workshops on maintaining a research-rich environment (1987) and on reforming introductory mathematics and science courses (1993). He currently serves as a mentor in PKAL's Faculty for the 21st Century program. He served as a founding member CUSE and is a co-author of its handbook, *Science Teaching Reconsidered*. He also served as president of the Council on Undergraduate Research from 1997-1998 and as chair of the Governing Board of the National Conferences on Undergraduate Research from 1990-1992.

George R. Boggs, *Palomar College,* is the superintendent/president of Palomar College, a comprehensive community college located in San Marcos, California. Dr. Boggs is a commissioner for the Accrediting Commission for Community and Junior Colleges of the Western Association of Schools and Colleges. He has served on the boards of directors of the California Association of Community Colleges, the Community College League of California, and the American Association of Community Colleges, where he was board chair in 1993/94. He is a member of the Advisory Committee for Education and Human Resources for the National Science Foundation (NSF) and has served on several NSF panels. Dr. Boggs is a former chemistry instructor. He is the author of more than 30 articles and chapters in professional journals and books.

Denice D. Denton, *University of Washington,* is the dean of engineering and a professor in the department of electrical engineering at the University of Washington. She received the B.S., M.S. (1982), and Ph.D. (1987) in electrical engineering from the Massachusetts Institute of Technology. Her current interests include plasma deposition of polymers and the use of micromachining in solid state actuator design. Professor Denton was co-director of the National Institute for Science Education in 1995-1996. She is a recipient of the National Science Foundation Presidential Young Investigator Award (1987-1992), the American Society of Engineering Education AT&T Foundation Teaching Award (1991), the W.M. Keck Foundation Engineering Teaching Excellence Award (1994), the American Society of Electrical Engineers George Westinghouse Award (1995), and the Institute of Electronic and Electrical Engineering Harriet B. Rigas Teaching Award (1995). Dr. Denton is the chair of the NRC's Board on Engineering Education.

Michael P. Doyle, *Research Corporation,* has served as the Dr. D.R. Semmes Distinguished Professor of Chemistry at Trinity University in San Antonio. He has received many awards for his work, including the Catalyst Award of the CMA and the ACS Award. Dr. Doyle is a member of the AAAS, the American Society of Biological Chemists, and the NIH.

Ramesh Gangolli, *University of Washington,* is professor of the mathematics department at the University of Washington. After receiving his Ph.D. in mathematics from the Massachusetts Institute of Technology and teaching there for two years, Dr. Gangolli has been a visiting professor at many institutions, in addition to his years at the University of Washington. He is widely published in the field of mathematics, and has received awards from the Sloan Fellowship and NSF, among other foundations, organizations, and agencies. He has served on the advisory committee on Mathematical Sciences for the NSF, and is associate editor of the *Journal of the Indian Mathematical Society.* Dr. Gangolli was a founding member of the CUSE.

Frederick T. Graybeal, *ASARCO Incorporated,* is chief geologist for ASARCO Incorporated, an international mining company. His responsibilities involve the worldwide review of geological environments for future exploration programs, introduction of new exploration concepts and technologies, and evaluation of acquisition opportunities. He worked previously for American and Canadian exploration companies and was an instructor for one year in the Department of Geology at the University of Arizona. He is a former vice president of the Society of Economic Geologists and serves on the advisory committee for the Department of Geosciences at the University of Arizona. Dr. Graybeal received an A.B. in geology from Dartmouth College in 1960 and M.S. (1962) and Ph.D. (1973) degrees in geology from the University of Arizona.

Norman Hackerman (NAS*), *The Robert A. Welch Foundation,* served as president of Rice University from 1970-1985 and holds the title of president emeritus and distinguished professor emeritus of chemistry at

Rice University. Prior to going to Rice, Dr. Hackerman spent 25 years at The University of Texas, Austin, where he joined the faculty as an assistant professor of chemistry in 1945 and progressed to president in 1967. He is now professor emeritus of chemistry at The University of Texas at Austin. He received his A.B. and Ph.D. degrees from Johns Hopkins University. He taught chemistry at Loyola College and Virginia Polytechnic and worked as a research chemist for Colloid Corporation, Kellex Corporation, and the U.S. Coast Guard. Dr. Hackerman was a member of the National Science Board from 1968 to 1980 and chairman from 1975 to 1980. He was the editor of the *Journal of the Electrochemical Society* from 1969 to 1989. He is a member of the National Academy of Sciences, the American Philosophical Society, and the American Academy of Arts and Sciences. He belongs to numerous scientific organizations. He is author or co-author of 225 publications. In addition to several previous awards, Dr. Hackerman received the American Institute of Chemists Gold Medal in March 1978, the Mirabeau B. Lamar Award of the Association of Texas College and Universities in 1981, the Distinguished Alumnus Award from Johns Hopkins University in 1982, Edward Goodrich Acheson Award of the Electrochemical Society in 1984, the Alumni Gold Medal for distinguished service to Rice University in 1984, Charles Lathrop Parsons Award of the American Chemical Society in 1987, the AAAS-Philip Hauge Abelson Prize in 1987, the Vannevar Bush Award of the National Science Board in 1993, and the National Medal of Science in 1993. Dr. Hackerman serves as chairman of the Scientific Advisory Board of The Robert A. Welch Foundation.

John K. Haynes, *Morehouse College,* serves as the David Packard Professor in Science and chair of Biology at Morehouse College. He received his B.S. from Morehouse in 1964 and his Ph.D. in Developmental Biology from Brown University in 1970. His research interests include regulation of cell volume in elasmobranchs and biochemical characterization of sickle cell membranes.

Eileen Delgado Johann, *Miami-Dade Community College,* is currently a professor of chemistry at Miami-Dade Community College, where she has been a full-time faculty member for 21 years. She has participated in numerous college activities, including the legislative committee and the student services committee. Dr. Johann has created interactive multimedia presentations in chemistry and nutrition and is the co-author of the nursing chemistry module series (inorganic, organic and biochemistry). Her professional affiliations include the Florida Association of Community Colleges, Two-Year College Chemistry Conference, American Chemical Society, and the College Hispanic Council.

William E. Kirwan, *Ohio State University,* is President of Ohio State University. Dr. Kirwan received his bachelor's degree from the University of Kentucky in 1960, and his master's and doctoral degrees from Rutgers in 1962 and 1964, respectively. He joined the University of Maryland as an assistant professor of mathematics in 1964. He was promoted to associate professor in 1968, to full professor in 1972, to chair of the Department of Mathematics in 1977, to vice chancellor for academic affairs in 1981, to provost in 1986, to acting president in August 1988, and to president in February 1989. During his tenure as president, the University of Maryland emphasized undergraduate education, selectively enhanced academic programs, recruited and retained distinguished faculty, achieved diversity goals for underrepresented minority groups, and successfully completed its first capital campaign. While serving as provost in the 1980s, Dr. Kirwan raised admissions standards, increased merit scholarships and graduate fellowships, and established an academic planning process. He is known for his long-range vision and for his talent as a consensus builder. Under his leadership, Maryland undertook a major restructuring of its academic organization, as well as streamlined its academic offerings, a move made necessary by reduced state support. Dr. Kirwan has regularly found time to teach an undergraduate class. Dr. Kirwan became President of the Ohio State University in 1998.

Sharon Long (NAS*), *Stanford University*, is an Investigator at the Howard Hughes Medical Institute and professor in the Department of Biological Science at Stanford University. Dr. Long is a leader in the identification and characterization of the genes in rhizobia that are involved in the nodulation of leguminous plants. Her group discovered that a flavone (lutiolin) derived from alfalfa seed extracts is necessary for activation of nodulation genes in *Rhizobium meliloti*. Dr. Long was elected as a member of the National Academy of Sciences in 1993.

Dorothy Merritts, *Franklin and Marshall College*, is chairperson of the environmental studies program and associate professor of geosciences for Franklin and Marshall College. Dr. Merritts has become nationally recognized for her research with undergraduate students and has received numerous grants from the National Science Foundation, Petroleum Research Fund, and U.S. Geological Survey to investigate earthquake and flooding processes in the western and central United States, Alaska, Indonesia, and Costa Rica. Dr. Merritts also has become nationally recognized as an advocate of science literacy at the introductory science course level. She recently completed a textbook in environmental geosciences that uses an Earth Systems approach, and has served on committees that promote the incorporation of an Earth Systems approach into the undergraduate curriculum. Most recently, she served on the NSF- and AGU-supported panel, "Spheres of Influence," which published a document regarding Earth Systems curricula for earth science educators. Dr. Merritts received a B.S. in geology, with minor in mathematics, from Indiana State University

in 1980, her M.S. in engineering geology from Stanford University in 1983, and her Ph.D. degree in tectonics, topography, and soils from University of Arizona in 1987.

John A. Moore (NAS*), *University of California at Riverside,* has an extensive history of involvement in educational activities. He began serving on National Research Council education committees in the 1950s and has continued to do so to this day. The more recent ones are the former Coordinating Council for Education, the CUSE, the Committee on Science Education K-12, the National Science Resources Center, and several committees related to NAS projects to produce materials for the K-12 teachers on the evolution/creationism problem. Beginning in the late 1950s, Dr. Moore worked with the Biological Sciences Curriculum Study, first as the chair of the Committee of the Content of the Curriculum Study, then as supervisor for the high school textbook, *Biological Science: An Inquiry into Life* (for two experimental versions and the first three commercial versions—1961-1973). Later, he worked on many other BSCS projects. Next, he worked on two experimental and three commercial editions of the middle school project, *Interactions of Man & the Biosphere* (1970-1979). For the university level, he has written *Principles of Zoology* (1957), *Heredity and Development* (1963, 1972), and *Readings in Heredity and Development* (1972). For the university level, he initiated and supervised the *Sciences as a Way of Knowing* project that consisted of seven yearly symposia and publications (1983-1989). Harvard University Press has published one volume, *Science as a Way of Knowing* based on this series (1993). For the graduate school level, he edited the 17 volumes of the series, *Genes, Cells and Organisms: Great Books in Experimental Biology*. He has served on many education committees of the National Science Foundation and the American Association for the Advancement of Science, including Project 2061. Dr. Moore received A.B., M.A., and Ph.D. degrees from

Columbia University and has taught at Brooklyn College, Queens College, Barnard College, Columbia University, and the University of California at Riverside.

Penny Moore, *Piedmont High School,* is a physics and mathematics teacher at Piedmont High School in Piedmont, California. She currently directs PRIME Science, an NSF-funded curriculum materials project that has published an integrated science curriculum for grades 6-10 (Kendall-Hunt). She directed Science for Science Teachers (SST), a program associated with the University of California at Berkeley (UCB) and supported by the National Science Foundation to prepare pre-college science teachers. She has held numerous positions as a presenter, speaker, demonstrator, and leader to address issues in pre-college teacher education. She has published articles on teacher education issues and has participated in several video projects on science education instruction. Ms. Moore earned a B.A. in physics from the University of California at Berkeley, and received her

California Life Secondary Teaching Credential at the UCB Graduate Internship Program. She is a member of several advisory boards and committees.

W. Ann Reynolds, *University of Alabama at Birmingham,* is President of the University of Alabama at Birmingham and served as Chancellor of the City University of New York (1990-1997) and as Chancellor of the California State University (1982-1990). Dr. Reynolds held academic rank at the University of California at Los Angeles School of Medicine, as clinical professor of obstetrics and gynecology, and at California State University-Dominguez Hills, as professor of biology. Dr. Reynolds has served on numerous boards, and received honorary degrees from universities that range from the University of Nebraska to Fu Jen Catholic University, Taiwan. She has published both papers and books in her field and is currently a member of the American Association for the Advancement of Science, the American Association of Anatomists, and the American Diabetes Association.

APPENDIX D
INTRODUCING THE *NATIONAL SCIENCE EDUCATION STANDARDS**

What are the National Science Education Standards*?*

The National Research Council released the *National Science Education Standards* in December of 1995. The *Standards* define the science content that all students should know and be able to do and provide guidelines for assessing the degree to which students have learned that content. The *Standards* detail the teaching strategies, professional development, and support necessary to deliver high quality science education to all students. The *Standards* also describe policies needed to bring coordination, consistency, and coherence to science education programs.

The National Science Education Standards *include standards for*

- **Content**
- **Teaching**
- **Assessment**
- **Professional Development**
- **Program**
- **System**

Why do we need the Standards*?*

- **Understanding science offers personal fulfillment and excitement.**
- **Citizens need scientific information and scientific ways of thinking in order to make informed decisions.**
- **Business and industry need entry-level workers with the ability to learn, reason, think creatively, make decisions, and solve problems.**

*National Research Council. 1997. Washington, DC: National Adademy Press; Available from National Academy Press, 1 (800) 624-6242. Mail your order to National Academy Press, 2101 Constitution Ave., NW, Lockbox 285, Washington, DC 20055.

- **Strong science and mathematics education can help our nation and individual citizens improve and maintain their economic productivity.**

Who developed the Standards?

Committees and working groups of scientists, teachers, and other educators appointed by the National Research Council developed the *Standards*. They engaged in a four-year process that involved review and critique by 22 science education and scientific organizations and broad state and local participation of over 18,000 individuals, including scientists, science educators, teachers, school administrators, and parents. The national consensus that resulted from this process gives the *Standards* a special credibility. Educators throughout the country who use them to inform changes in science education programs can be assured that the *Standards* represent the highest quality thinking this country can provide its citizens.

The vision of the Standards:

All students, regardless of age, gender, cultural or ethnic background, disabilities, aspirations, or interest and motivation in science, should have the opportunity to attain high levels of scientific literacy.

Guiding Principles behind the Standards

- **Science is for all students.**
- **Learning science is an active process.**
- **School science reflects traditions of contemporary science.**
- **Improving science is part of systemwide educational reform.**

How do students learn science?

The *Standards* are based on the premise that learning science is something that students do, not something that is done to them. The *Standards* envision an active learning process in which students describe objects and events, ask questions, formulate explanations, test those explanations, and communicate their ideas to others. In this way, students build strong knowledge of science content, apply that knowledge to new problems, learn how to communicate clearly, and build critical and logical thinking skills.

Through their study of science, students

- **Experience the richness and excitement of the natural world**
- **Apply scientific principles and processes to make personal decisions**
- **Discuss matters of scientific and technological concern**
- **Increase their potential contribution to society and to the economy**

What should students know and be able to do?

The **Content Standards** describe the knowledge and abilities students need to develop, from kindergarten through high school, in order to become scientifically literate.

What is scientific literacy?   Scientific literacy is the knowledge and understanding of scientific concepts and processes required for personal decision making, participation in civic and cultural affairs, and economic productivity. People who are scientifically literate can ask, find, or determine answers to questions about everyday experiences. They are able to describe, explain, and predict natural phenomena.

Scientific literacy has different degrees and forms; it expands and deepens over a lifetime, not just during the years in school. The *Standards* outline a broad base of knowledge and skills for a lifetime of continued development in scientific literacy for every citizen, as well as provide a foundation for those aspiring to scientific careers.

How are the National Science Education Standards different from the American Association for the Advancement of Science's Benchmarks for Science Literacy?

The documents differ in three ways. First, they divide content by different grade levels. The *Benchmarks* are statements of what all students should know and be able to do in science, mathematics, and technology by the end of grades 2, 5, 8, and 12; the *Standards* use grades 4, 8, and 12 as end points. Second, the *Standards* place greater emphasis on inquiry, including it as important science content as well as a means of teaching and learning. Third, the *Standards* offer a broader set of standards for improving science education. They address all components of education, including teaching, assessment, professional development, program, and system, recognizing that improvement cannot occur or be sustained in one segment of the system alone. There is, however, a high level of consistency between the two documents in describing the content to be learned. The National

Research Council believes that the use of the *Benchmarks* complies fully with the spirit of the content standards.

What is included in content standards?

Content standards are divided into eight categories:

- **Unifying concepts and processes**
- **Science as inquiry**
- **Physical science**
- **Life science**
- **Earth and space science**
- **Science and technology**
- **Science in personal and social perspectives**
- **History and nature of science**

The content standards include traditional school science content but, in addition, encompass other knowledge and abilities of scientists. The first category of the content standards, unifying concepts and processes, identifies powerful ideas that are basic to the science disciplines and help students of all ages understand the natural world. This category is presented for all grade levels because the concepts are developed throughout a student's education. The other content categories are clustered for grades K-4, 5-8, and 9-12. Students develop knowledge and abilities in inquiry, which ground their learning of subject matter in physical, life, and earth and space sciences. Science and technology standards link the natural and designed worlds. The personal and social perspectives standards help students see the personal and social impacts of science and help them develop decision-making skills. The history and nature of science standards help students see science as a human experience that is on-going and ever-changing.

What do teachers of science do?

The **Teaching Standards** provide an answer to this question. Science teaching lies at the heart of the vision of science education presented in the *Standards*. Effective teachers of science have theoretical and practical knowledge about student learning, science, and science teaching. The teaching standards describe actions these teachers take and skills and knowledge they have to teach science well.

CONTENT STANDARDS

	Grades K-4	Grades 5-8	Grades 9-12
Unifying Concepts and Processes	Systems, order, and organization Evidence, models, and explanation Change, constancy, and measurement Evolution and equilibrium Form and function	Systems, order, and organization Evidence, models, and explanation Change, constancy, and measurement Evolution and equilibrium Form and function	Systems, order, and organization Evidence, models, and explanation Change, constancy, and measurement Evolution and equilibrium Form and function
Science as Inquiry	Abilities necessary to do scientific inquiry Understandings about scientific inquiry	Abilities necessary to do scientific inquiry Understandings about scientific inquiry	Abilities necessary to do scientific inquiry Understandings about scientific inquiry
Physical Science	Properties of objects and materials Position and motion of objects Light, heat, electricity, and magnetism	Properties and changes of properties in matter Motions and forces Transfer of energy	Structure of atoms Structure and properties of matter Chemical reactions Motions and forces Conservation of energy and increase in disorder Interactions of energy and matter
Life Science	Characteristics of organisms Life cycles of organisms Organisms and environments	Structure and function in living systems Reproduction and heredity Regulation and behavior Populations and ecosystems Diversity and adaptations of organisms	The cell Molecular basis of heredity Biological evolution Interdependence of organisms Matter, energy, and organization in living systems Behavior of organisms
Earth and Space Science	Properties of earth materials Objects in the sky Changes in earth and sky	Structure of the earth system Earth's history Earth in the solar system	Energy in the earth system Geochemical cycles Origin and evolution of the earth system Origin and evolution of the universe
Science and Technology	Abilities of technological design Understandings about science and technology Abilities to distinguish between natural objects and objects made by humans	Abilities of technological design Understandings about science and technology	Abilities of technological design Understandings about science and technology
Science in Personal and Social Perspectives	Personal health Characteristics and changes in populations Types of resources Changes in environments Science and technology in local challenges	Personal health Populations, resources, and environments Natural hazards Risks and benefits Science and technology in society	Personal and community health Population growth Natural resources Environmental quality Natural and human-induced hazards Science and technology in local, national, and global challenges
History and Nature of Science	Science as a human endeavor	Science as a human endeavor Nature of science History of science	Science as a human endeavor Nature of scientific knowledge Historical perspectives

Teachers of science

- **Plan an inquiry-based science program**
- **Guide and facilitate learning**
- **Assess student learning and their own teaching**
- **Design and manage learning environments**
- **Develop communities of science learners**
- **Participate in on-going development of the school science program**

How can teachers apply the* Standards *in their classrooms? Individual teachers are encouraged by the *Standards* to give less emphasis to fact-based programs and greater emphasis to inquiry-based programs that engage students in an in-depth study of fewer topics. However, to attain the vision of science education described in the *Standards*, more than teaching practices and materials must change. The routines, rewards, structures, and expectations of districts, schools, and other parts of the system must endorse the vision, and provide teachers with resources, time, and opportunities to change their practice. Teachers can use the program and system standards to communicate this need to administrators and parents.

How is science learning assessed?

The **Assessment Standards** provide criteria to judge progress across the system toward the science education vision of scientific literacy for all. They can be used in preparing evaluations of students, teachers, programs, and policies.

Assessments should

- **Be deliberately designed for the decisions they are intended to inform**
- **Measure both achievement and opportunity to learn**
- **Clearly relate decisions to data**
- **Demonstrate fairness in design and use**
- **Support their inferences with data**

Will the* Standards *help teachers test their students more effectively? Teaching and testing are integral components of instruction, and cannot be separated. As content and teaching strategies become aligned with the *Standards*, so must classroom assessments. The assessment standards identify essential characteristics of effective assessment policies, practices, and tasks at all levels. Teachers who use the standards will think differently about what to assess, when to do so, and the best ways to determine what their students are learning. They will consider carefully the fundamental understandings their students are working to learn, the place their students are in developing understanding, and a variety of alternatives to help their students demonstrate what they know.

Will standardized tests change? The *Standards* address the need for systems to reconsider the purpose, data analysis, and sample size in all large-scale assessments. There are already indications that changes in items on common standardized tests are being considered, as are the designs used by states, districts, and others who conduct large-scale science assessments.

What do teachers need to know and how will they learn it?

The **Professional Development Standards** make the case that becoming an effective teacher of science is a continuous process, stretching from preservice throughout one's professional career. The professional development standards can be used to help teachers of K-12 science have the on-going, in-depth kinds of learning opportunities that are required by and available to all professionals.

Professional Development Standards call for teachers to have opportunities to

- **Learn science through inquiry**
- **Integrate knowledge of science, learning, and teaching**
- **Engage in continuous reflection and improvement**
- **Build coherent, coordinated programs for professional learning**

How will teachers gain the science content knowledge they need?

To help their students achieve high levels of science literacy, teachers need to understand deeply the content they teach. Building science knowledge

- **Involves active investigation**
- **Focuses on significant science**
- **Uses scientific literature and technology**

- **Builds on teachers' current knowledge**
- **Encourages on-going reflection**
- **Supports collaboration among teachers**

How will teachers improve their science teaching? Effective teachers of science have specialized knowledge that combines their understanding of science with what they know about learning, teaching, curriculum, and students. They develop this unique type of knowledge through both preservice and inservice learning experiences that

- **Deliberately connect science and pedagogy**
- **Model effective teaching practices**
- **Address the needs of teachers as adult learners**
- **Take place in classrooms and other learning situations**
- **Use inquiry, reflection, research, modeling, and guided practice**

What is an effective school science program?

The **Program Standards** address the need for comprehensive and coordinated science experiences across grade levels and support needed by teachers in order for all students to have opportunities to learn. The program standards will help schools and districts translate the *Standards* into effective programs that reflect local contexts and policies.

Program Standards call for
- **Consistency across all elements of the science program and across K-12**
- **Quality in the program of studies**
- **Coordination with mathematics**
- **Quality resources–teachers, time, materials**
- **Equitable opportunities for achievement**
- **Collaboration within the school community to support a quality program**

Quality Programs of Study
- **Include all content standards**
- **Select developmentally appropriate content**
- **Emphasize student understanding through inquiry**
- **Connect science to other subjects**

Are the* Standards *a science curriculum? Curriculum is the way content is designed and delivered. It includes the structure, organization, balance, and presentation of the content in the classroom. The *Standards* do not prescribe a specific curriculum but, rather, provide criteria that can be used at the local, state, and national levels to design a curriculum framework, a key element in a school or district's science program, or to evaluate and select curriculum materials. Effective science programs are designed to consider and draw consistency from the content, teaching, and assessment standards, as well as professional development, program, and system standards.

How does the system support science learning?

The **System Standards** call on all parts of the educational system—including local districts, state departments of education, and the federal education system—to coordinate their efforts and build on one another's strengths. The standards can serve as criteria for judging the performance of components of the system responsible for providing schools with necessary financial and intellectual resources.

System Standards require

- **Policies consistent with vision of the *Standards***
- **Coordination of policies within and across system**
- **Continuity of support over time**
- **Sufficient resources to support program**
- **Equitable policies**
- **Attention to anticipated effects**
- **Individual responsibility for achieving the vision**

The road ahead. The changes required to achieve the vision of the *Standards* are substantial and will take well into the 21st century. No one group can implement them. The challenge of a *Standards*-based science program extends to everyone within the education community. Change will occur locally, and differences in individuals, schools, and communities will result in different pathways to improvement, different rates of progress, and different school science programs. What is important is that change be pervasive and sustainable, leading to high quality science education for **all** students.